A practical introduction to
to
Microsoft Office 97

GW00597367

OTHER TITLES OF INTEREST

A practical introduction to Microsoft Office 97

By

David Weale

BERNARD BABANI (publishing) LTD
THE GRAMPIANS
SHEPHERDS BUSH ROAD
LONDON W6 7NF
ENGLAND

PLEASE NOTE

Although every care has been taken with the production of this book to ensure that any instructions or any of the other contents operate in a correct and safe manner, the Author and the Publishers do not accept any responsibility for any failure, damage or loss caused by following the said contents. The Author and Publisher do not take any responsibility for errors or omissions.

The Author and Publisher make no warranty or representation, either express or implied, with respect to the contents of this book, its quality, merchantability or fitness for a particular purpose.

The Author and Publisher will not be liable to the purchaser or to any other person or legal entity with respect to any liability, loss or damage (whether direct, indirect, special, incidental or consequential) caused or alleged to be caused directly or indirectly by this book.

The book is sold as is, without any warranty of any kind, either expressed or implied, respecting the contents, including but not limited to implied warranties regarding the book's quality, performance, correctness or fitness for any particular purpose.

No part of this book may be reproduced or copied by any means whatever without written permission of the publisher.

All rights reserved

© 1998 BERNARD BABANI (publishing) LTD

Screen Shot(s) reprinted with permission from Microsoft® Corporation
First Published - August 1998
British Library Cataloguing in Publication Data
A catalogue record for this book is available from the British Library

ISBN 0 85934 452 5
Cover Design by Gregor Arthur
Cover Illustration by Adam Willis
Printed and bound in Great Britain by Cox & Wyman Ltd, Reading

Preface

Welcome to Microsoft® Office 97.

I wrote this book to help you in learning how to use Office 97 practically. It is intended to explain the program in a way that I hope you will find useful, and that you will learn by doing.

Each section of the book covers a different aspect of the program and contains various hints and tips which I have found useful and may enhance your work.

By working through the material and practising it, you will build up an expertise in the use of the applications.

The text is written both for the new user and for the more experienced person who wants an easy to follow reference.

Please note that you should know how to use the basic techniques of Microsoft® Windows® 95; if you do not, there are many excellent texts on the subject.

I hope you learn from this book and have fun doing so.

With best wishes

David Weale, July 1998

TRADEMARKS

Microsoft®, MS-DOS® and Windows® are registered trademarks of Microsoft® Corporation.

All other trademarks are the registered and legally protected trademarks of the companies who make the products. There is no intent to use the trademarks generally and readers should investigate ownership of a trademark before using it for any purpose.

ABOUT THE AUTHOR

David Weale is a Fellow of the Institute of Chartered Accountants and has worked in both private and public practice.

At present, he is a lecturer in business computing at Yeovil College.

He lives in Somerset with his wife, three children and two cats.

DEDICATION

This is for everyone who strives to learn, I wish you well.

Contents

Word

Text entry and saving files

Please type in the following text.

Do **not** use the **Return** key until the end of the paragraph.

See how any spelling mistakes are identified with red underlining and grammar errors with green underlining. Do **not** correct them at present.

You should leave **only** a single space after commas or full stops.

```
Word for Windows is a word processing program
that is intuitive in use. It can be used in a
simple way and can be used in a very
sophisticated way, with the available features
resembling those of a major desktop publishing
program. Word for Windows is in many ways
easier to use than a DTP program especially for
the non-professional.
```

Save the file, by clicking on the **Save** button on the toolbar.

The **Save As** dialog box will be displayed, call your file TEST and save it in the appropriate folder.

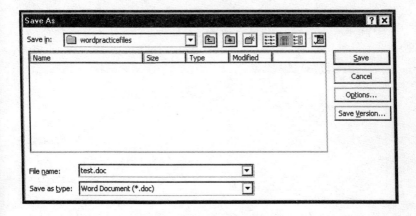

Close the file (pull down the **File** menu and select **Close**).

Opening files and adding text

To open the file, click the **Open** button and then select the file you want to open and click on the **Open** button (or double-click the filename).

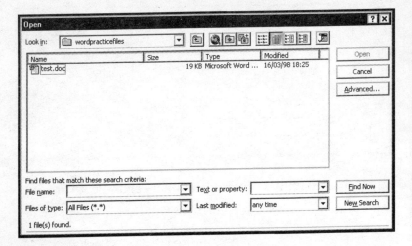

Move the cursor to the end of the text (**Ctrl** and **End**).

Return twice to create a blank line and then on the next line enter the new text (you should end up with two paragraphs with a blank line between them).

```
During the course you will be learning how to
use W4W, starting with the basic features of
text entry and saving files. Then you will move
on to learn how to edit and format the text,
how to align text, how to insert and delete
text and how to spell check your work (very
useful).
```

Save the file by clicking on the **Save** button on the toolbar and then enter the following text in the same way.

```
After having learnt and practised these, you
will move on to techniques such as cut and
paste, how to use bullets and numbered
paragraphs and how to indent.

Other topics that will be covered include
borders and shading, headers and footers and
creating tables. Incorporating pictures will
also be looked at.
```

You should now have four separate paragraphs.

Save the file.

Your screen should look similar to this.

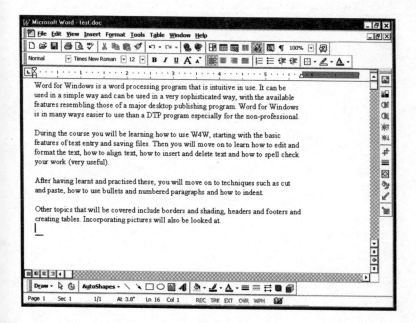

Editing text

Inevitably you will want to edit (alter) the text.

Move the cursor to the end of the second sentence (first paragraph) and enter the following as a new sentence (spelt as shown). The rest of the text will move to make space.

```
Ffor exampel you cann use frames to manippulate
the pictures in various ways.
```

If you need to delete text, click the mouse at the start or end of the words and (keeping the mouse button depressed) move the mouse across the words until all are highlighted and then press the **Delete** key on the keyboard.

Move the cursor to the end of the first paragraph and delete the last four words (so that the final word within the paragraph is `program`) and save the file.

Previewing your work

Modern word processing programs have a preview feature that lets you see how the text will look **before** printing it out. This saves both time and paper.

Click on the **Preview** button on the toolbar and you will see the text shown as it will be printed out.

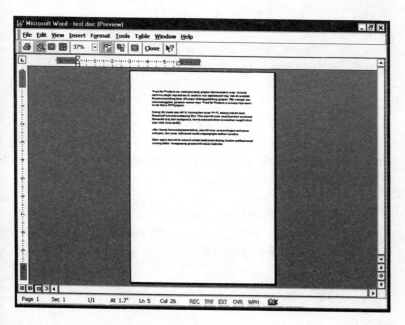

Note the **multiple page preview** button and the **Zoom** feature. By clicking on these, you can alter the number of pages and size of the page(s). Click on the **Close** button to return to the previous screen.

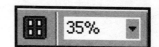

Alignment

Position the cursor within the first paragraph and then click on the **Justify** button. Notice the effect, the right hand margin will be straight.

Position the cursor within the second paragraph and click on the **Center** button.

Position the cursor within the third paragraph and click on the **Align Right** button. Look at how the text is laid out on the page by previewing it.

Highlight all the text (by clicking the mouse at the start of the text and holding down the mouse button, drag the mouse over the text, letting go **only** when the required area is highlighted).

Click on the **Justify** button, and look at how the text is laid out on the page by previewing it (the right hand margin of the text should be straight) as you can see from the illustration.

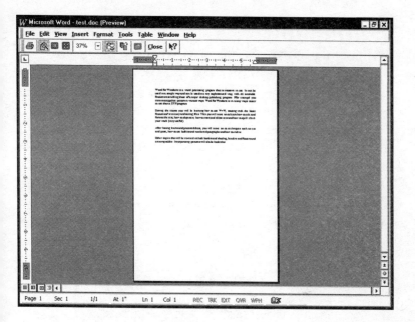

Save the file.

Formatting

Position the cursor at the very start of the page (**Ctrl Home**) and use the **Return** key to create two blank lines at the top of the page. Move the cursor to the very top and enter the following title.

```
Learning WORD
```

Highlight the title then click on the **Bold** button on the toolbar, and then highlight (the word) WORD and pull down the **Format** menu, select **Font** and colour it red.

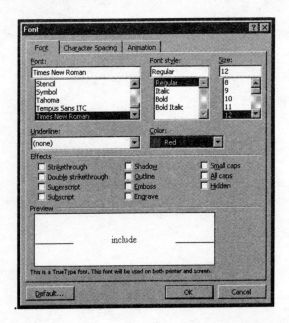

Alternatively, you can click the arrow to the right of the **Font Color** button to select a colour.

With the title still highlighted, click on the **Font** display (specifically the arrow to the right of the font name) and from the resulting list of fonts choose ARIAL.

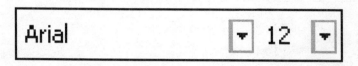

Do the same with the **Font Size**, this time selecting 20.

The title should now stand out from the text.

Finally, centre the title.

Click within the last paragraph and while holding down the **Ctrl** key press the number 2 key above the QWERTY keys. This should double-space the paragraph.

Repeat this process only this time use **Ctrl** and the number **1** key, the text should revert to single line spacing.

Your file should look like this when previewed.

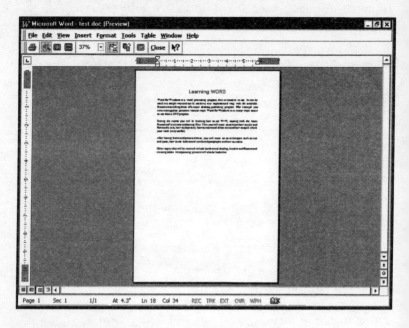

Save the file (with the same name) and close it.

Page Breaks

Open the file TEST.

WORD automatically sets page breaks (i.e. where a new page starts). You may want to alter these, for example the program may put a page break in the middle of a paragraph (it is normally thought poor layout to have one or two lines of a paragraph ending up on the preceding or following page).

To set **page breaks** position the cursor where you want the page break to appear and then press the **Return** key while holding down the **Ctrl** key. You will see a dotted line appear across the page, this shows a page break.

To remove a page break, position the cursor on the dotted line and press the **Delete** key.

Put a page break between paragraph one and paragraph two and another between paragraph two and paragraph three.

Move the cursor to the top of the file and preview the file. You should see that it now extends to three separate pages.

Remove the page breaks and preview the file again to make sure that it is now all on one page. Close the file (**File Close**) **without** saving the changes.

Spell and grammar checking

Inevitably you will type some words incorrectly and having access to a spell checker is very useful.

Open the file (TEST) and make sure that the cursor is at the top of the page.

Click on the spell-checking button.

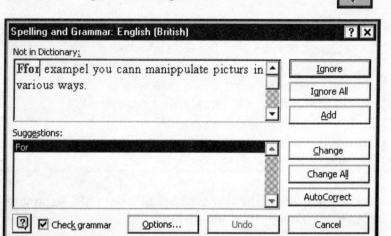

You can **Add** to the dictionary (inevitably the dictionary is finite in size and a word may be correct but be identified by the spell checker since it is not in the dictionary).

Change the words as necessary by clicking on the **Change** button and then **Save** the file.

This version of WORD also checks your grammar!

Moving text (cut & paste)

After entering the data, you may want to move some of the text around.

There are several ways to do this; the one you are going to use is the standard Windows technique of **Cut & Paste**.

This technique is common to all Windows applications and can be used both within one application and between applications (for example to copy a picture from PowerPoint® to W4W).

Highlight the second paragraph.

Click on the **Cut** button and the text will be cut from your document (it is held in the Windows **Clipboard**).

Move the cursor to the end of the document (**Returning** if necessary to create a blank line).

Click on the **Paste** button and the paragraph you cut will reappear.

If there is too much or too little space between the paragraphs, use the **Return** or **Delete** keys as necessary.

Now cut the first paragraph and paste it below the last (to practise the technique).

Preview the file and then **Save** it.

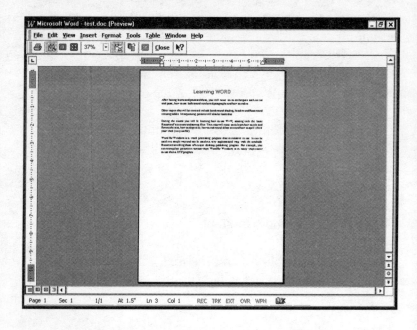

Borders

One way of making text stand out is to place a border around it; this border can be shaded (filled with a pattern) if you wish.

Highlight the third paragraph, pull down the **Format** menu, and select **Borders and Shading**.

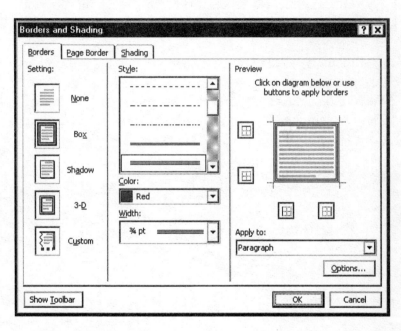

Choose the border **Style**, **Color** and **Width** you want, make sure that the **Apply To** box shows the word **Paragraph**. Finally, click on **Box** and then on **OK**

You should now have a border around the text.

Repeat this operation for the first paragraph using a different type of border.

Now highlight each bordered paragraph (in turn) and use the arrow to the right of the **Border** button on the toolbar.

Click on the button with no border shown. The borders should have disappeared.

You can use the **F4** function key to repeat the previous formatting command.

Finally place a shadowed border around the title, check that you have highlighted just the title and that the **Apply To** box displays **Text**) and this time also select **Shading**. Choose a suitable **Pattern Style** and **Color** (again ensuring that the **Apply To** box shows **Text**).

Preview the result and **Save** the file.

Indenting

Another method of making text stand out is to use a technique called Indents.

Highlight the third paragraph and then pull down the **Format** menu. Select **Paragraph** and then **Indents and Spacing**, enter the figures 2" for both left and right indents within the dialog box that appears.

To alter the measurements from centimetres to inches, pull down the **Tools** menu and select **Options** and then **General**. You will see the **Measurement units** at the bottom of this box.

Indent the first paragraph by 3" (left indent only).

Preview the file and you will see the way the indented paragraphs stands out.

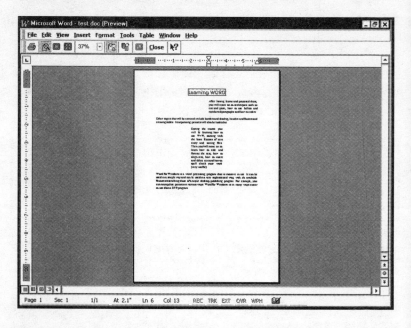

Remove the paragraph indents for paragraphs one and three by highlighting the paragraphs and resetting the left and right indents to zero (remember you can use the **F4** key to repeat formatting).

Save the file.

Headers & Footers

These give a professional look to a document; headers and footers are text (or pictures) that appear at the top or bottom of each page.

Pull down the **View** menu and select **Header and Footer**. The toolbar will be displayed.

Switch to the **Footer** by clicking on the **Switch** button

You will see the screen alter so that a footer section appears in the lower part of the screen.

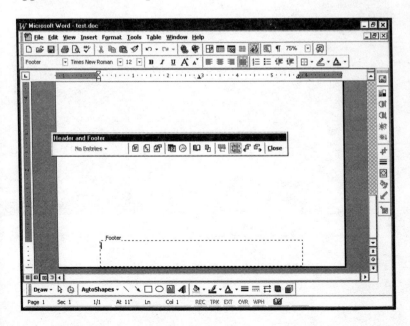

Enter the page number by clicking on the page number button.

Change the font to italic and two points smaller than the rest of the text. Finally, right align it.

Close the footer window and preview your text, you should see the footer at the bottom of the page.

Add your name as a header; format it to italic, two points smaller than the text and left aligned.

Preview and save the file.

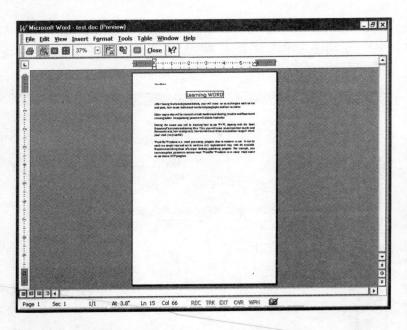

You can add any text, date or symbols to the header or footer.

To add a date pull down the **Insert** menus and select **Date and Time** (this gives more choice than using the **Date** button in the toolbar).

To insert a symbol (for example a copyright symbol ©), pull down the **Insert** menu and select **Symbol**).

Printing

You have learnt how to preview your work, printing it out is almost as simple.

You have two options when you print.

Use the **Print** button on the toolbar. This will print to the default printer.

Pull down the **File** menu and then **Print**. This option both allows you to change the printer and to select the number of copies and so on.

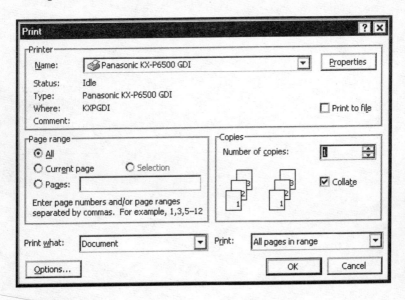

Print your file if you wish.

Close the file.

Numbering paragraphs

Open the file TEST and position the cursor in the first paragraph and then click on the **Numbering** button.

The paragraph will be numbered and indented automatically.

Highlight the other paragraphs and click on the **Numbering** button, the numbers should be sequential.

Preview the file and then save it as TESTNUM (remember to pull down the **File** menu and choose **Save As**).

Tip: If the numbering does not start with the correct figure then (after highlighting all the paragraphs) pull down the **Format** menu and select **Bullets** and **Numbering**. Within this dialog box choose **Customise** and there is an option called **Start at**. You can change the number to any number you wish.

Bullets

A similar technique to numbering, bullets puts a symbol instead of a number at the start of the paragraph (which is indented in the same way as the numbered paragraphs).

Highlight all the numbered paragraphs and click on the **Bullet** button.

Pull down the **Format** menu, and select **Bullets and Numbering.**

Choose another of the bullets and then click on OK. You should now have bulleted paragraphs in place of the numbered ones.

Preview and then save the file (**File** and **Save As**) as TESTBULL.

By using the **Format** and **Bullets** followed by **Customise** and then **Bullet** you can alter the bullets, some of the most original bullets are found in the **Wingdings**® font set.

Close the file.

Search and replace

It is sometimes necessary to search for a specific word and to replace it with another word. This is a technique common to all word processing programs.

Open the file TEST and move the cursor to the top of the file (a quick way of doing this is to hold the **Ctrl** key and while doing so to press the **Home** key). Pull down the **Edit** menu and select **Replace**.

Enter the word to in the **Find what** box and the word three in the **Replace with** box.

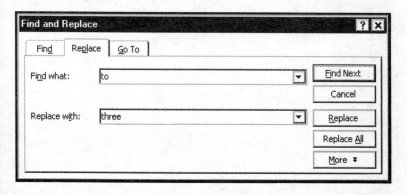

Click on the **Replace All** button and all the occurrences of the word to will be replaced with the word three.

I am sure that since the text is now not making much sense you will want to change it back!

Close the file, without saving the changes.

Inserting clipart

It is easy to add graphics to your work.

Open the file TEST and position the cursor between the second and third paragraphs.

Pull down the **Insert** menu and select **Picture** then **Clip Art**. You will see the **Microsoft Clip Gallery**. Choose **Clip Art** (if necessary).

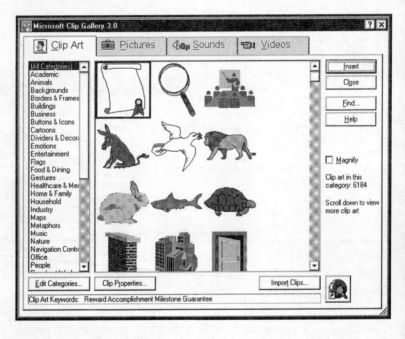

Within this there are many pictures, select one. Insert your chosen picture into the document.

WORD 97 treats pictures rather differently from previous versions and you will need to position the picture by pulling down the **Format** menu and selecting **Picture** and then **Size**, alter the **Height** to 1" and then click in the **Width** box to (automatically) adjust the width. Now select **Wrapping**.

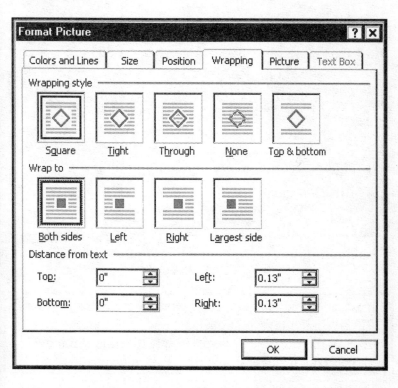

Choose **Square** Wrapping style and **Wrap to Both sides** (as shown above). You will see the text wrap around the picture.

Drag the picture to the middle of the page.

Preview and save the file as TESTFR (**File** and **Save As**).
It may look similar to this.

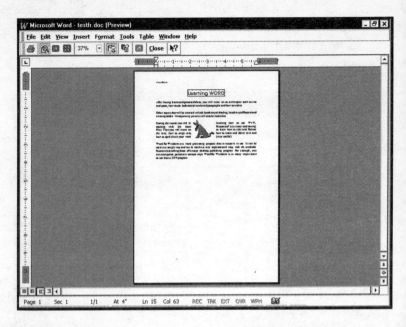

Close the file.

Please note that it is not good practice to use a graphic to
split a single text column into two. It makes reading
difficult, the exercise is purely to practice the technique of
wrapping not to suggest that this is good layout.

Word Art

Another feature of W4W is **Word Art**. This can be used for logos or any other situation where you want to use fancy lettering.

Open the file TEST and position the cursor just below the title and then pull down the **Insert** menu and select **Object**.

From the list, choose **Microsoft Word Art 3**. You will see the **Word Art** module appear.

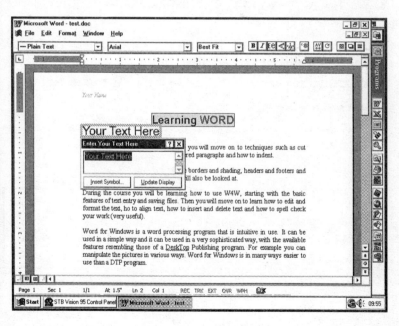

Enter the following (returning at the end of each line).

```
Your Name
Telephone number
```

Choose a suitable shape, font, colour, fill, effect, etc., from the selections shown along the toolbar (see below) and click outside the dialog box when finished.

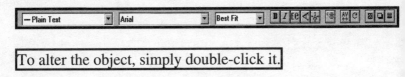

To alter the object, simply double-click it.

Once the **Word Art** object is embedded into your document, you can size it to taste and position it.

Select the Word Art object by clicking on it.

Pull down the **Format** menu, then **Object** and **Position** (check that **Float over text** is ticked), then select **Wrapping**, **Square Wrapping** style and **Wrap to Right**.

Also adjust the measurements **Distance From Text** until it looks similar to that shown below.

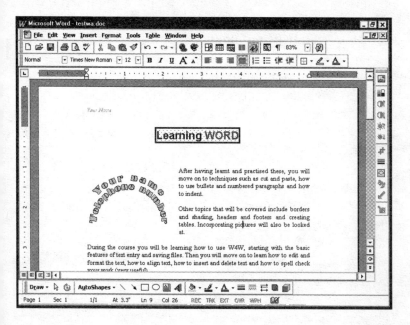

Save the file as TESTWA.

Altering graphic alignment

At present the **Word Art** object is set to **Float over text**. This means that the graphic can be positioned anywhere on the page, simply by dragging and positioning it.

If you want to align it to the left, centre or right then you need to click the cursor on the picture and then pull down the **Format** menu and select **Object**. Now choose **Position** and click on the **Float over text** so that there is **no** tick in the box.

Do this for the **Word Art** object and centre the picture by clicking on the **Centre** button. Put a thick border around the picture and centre it.

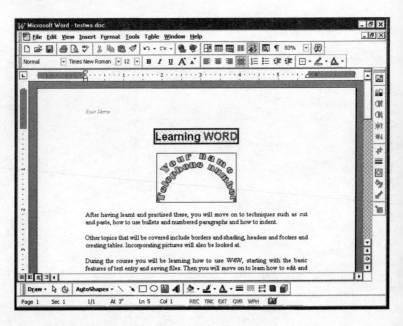

Save the file as TESTFX and close the file.

Counting the number of words

There is often a requirement to know how many words have been used in a document. This is easy in W4W.

Open the file TEST

Pull down the **Tools** menu and select **Word Count** and there it is!

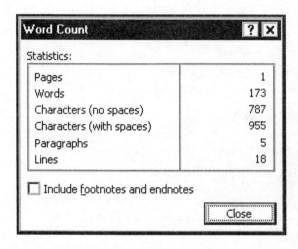

Page Setup

You may want to customise the paper size or the margins for specific pieces of work. The various options (all of which use the **File** and then **Page Setup** commands) are:

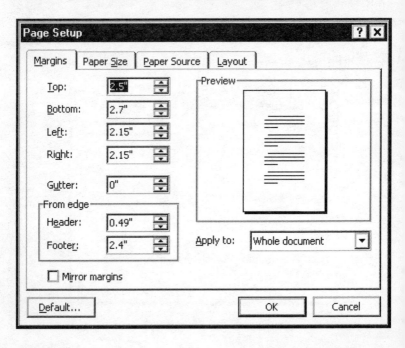

Margins, you can alter the margins for all the text (be careful to distinguish between this technique and indenting which can be applied to individual paragraphs).

Paper Size, here you can change between **Portrait** and **Landscape** orientation and alter the paper size (printers normally use A4).

Close the file.

Adding Footnotes

Academics often add footnotes to their work to explain words within the text or to clarify. This is very easy to do.

Open TESTBULL.

Place the cursor after the phrase W4W (third paragraph) and pull down the **Insert** menu, select **Footnote** and **OK**.

The footnote screen will be displayed. Type in a footnote (Word for Windows).

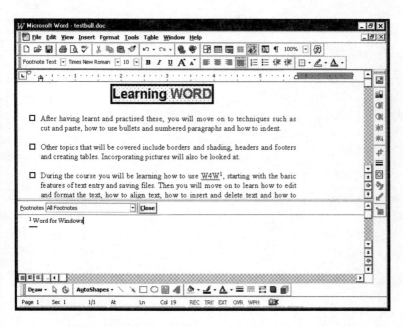

Close the footnote section and then preview the file to see how it looks.

Changing Case

There is a very quick and easy method of changing the case of any character.

Highlight the title, then hold down the **Shift** key, and press the **F3** function key. Repeat this until you have the combination of upper and lower case characters you want.

Now see how **Format** followed by **Change Case** works.

Save the file as TESTBULL and close it.

Creating columns

Open the file TEST; highlight all the text (only), and copy it below itself (twice) using the **copy** button and then the **paste** button (so there is three times as much text as originally).

Pull down the **View** menu and select **Page Layout**.

Click on the **Columns** button in the toolbar and highlight two columns. Your document will now be in two columns, which you can see by previewing the file.

After previewing the text, you may see that the title is slightly strange and is not centred. If this is the case, position the cursor just below the title and pull down the **Insert** menu and then **Break**, finally selecting **Continuous Section Break**. Position the cursor in the title section and using the **Column** button select single columns and then centre the title.

Insert a **Column Break** (**Insert Break**) before the last paragraph in the initial column and then use the **Return** key to line up the columns.

Finally put a page break just before the last paragraph in the second column.

Preview the file to see it is ok and then save it (**File** and **Save As**) as COLTEST and close it.

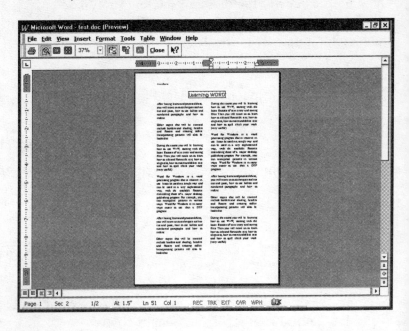

Tables

The more sophisticated word processing programs have a feature called **Tables**. This helps in laying out columns of words or figures symmetrically.

Create a new file using the **New File** button or by pulling down the **File** menu and selecting **New**.

Click on the **Insert Table** button and highlight a grid of four rows (down) by three columns (across). Enter the following data into the table (using the **Tab** key to move between cells).

Week	Activity	Topic
1	Lecture	The Purposes of Accounting
2	Lecture/ Practice	Cash Flow Statements
3 - 5	Lecture/ Practice	Double Entry Book-keeping

Highlight the table. Click on the **Format** menu and then on **Borders and Shading**. Choose the line style and then click on the **Grid** symbol.

At this stage it is best to be in **Page Layout View** (**View** menu).

Highlight the top row and format the text to bold and alter the column widths of the table as necessary by positioning the mouse pointer on the line dividing two columns and then clicking and dragging the line.

You should now have a table with the grid lines showing when you preview the file. Save the file as TEST1.

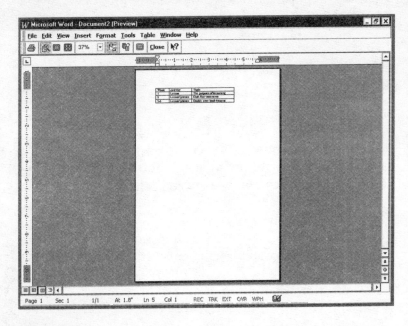

Position the cursor in the very last cell of the table and use the **Tab** key to add another row to the table.

Add the following text and preview and save the file

6 - 7	Lecture/ Practice	Profit & Loss Accounts

Now add the following column to the table. To do this, position the cursor just beyond the last column and then pull down the **Table** menu and **Select Column** followed by **Insert Columns**.

Chapter
1-2
Handout
3
4

Centre align the fourth (new) column and alter the column widths as appropriate.

Highlight the top row of the table and add a shaded pattern to it and a thicker border.

Change the **Page Setup** to **Landscape**, preview and save the file as TEST1. Close the file.

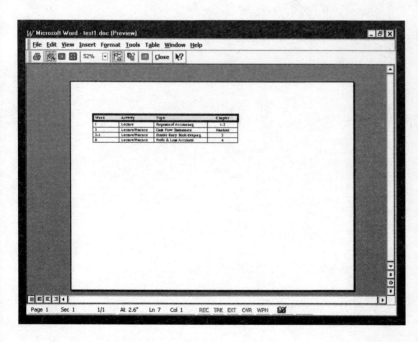

Text Styles

In order to achieve consistency and to enable you to automatically produce a TOC (table of contents) you can use the **Styles** feature.

Open the file TEST.

Add headings to each of the paragraphs, giving them the name Paragraph One, Paragraph Two and so on.

Now click on the first heading and then on the **Style** button on the toolbar (to the left of the font button), click on the arrow to the right.

This pulls down a list.

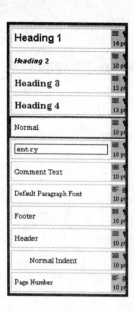

Select **Heading 1** style for the first paragraph heading and then **Heading 2** for the second, **Heading 1** for the third and **Heading 2** for the fourth.

You can see how it may look in the following illustration.

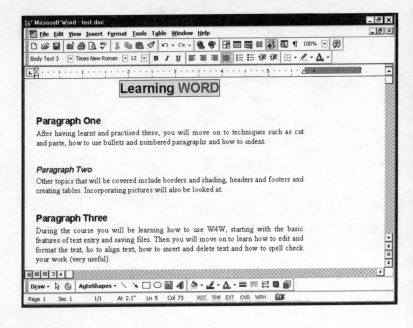

Altering styles

You can alter any style, for example highlight an example of **Heading 1** style.

Pull down the **Format** menu and select **Style**. You will see the following dialog box.

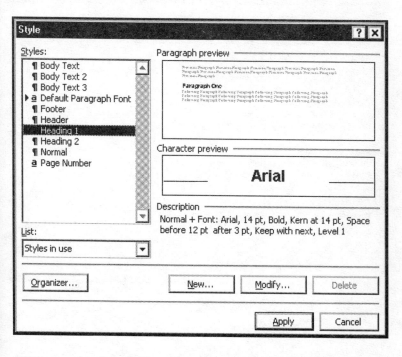

Click on the **Modify** button and then select **Format** and then **Font**. Alter the font type (to **Baskerville Old Face**), the size (to 16 pt) and colour (to **red**) and click on the **OK** button.

On the next screen make sure the **Automatically Update** box is checked and click on **OK** and then on **Apply**.

All the examples of **Heading 1** style will have changed.

To practise, change the style of the other heading's style.

It may look similar to this.

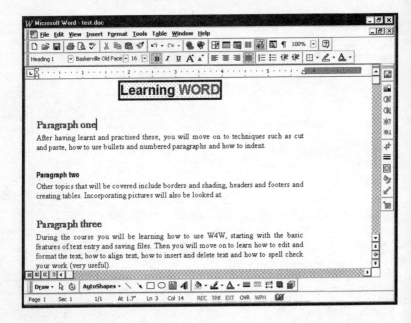

TOC (table of contents)

Insert a **Page Break** before each of the paragraphs (including the first).

Position the cursor at the top of the file (just below the title).

Type in the word Contents and format it to Arial 16 point.

Create a table of contents by pulling down the **Insert** menu, followed by **Index and Tables** and finally **Table Of Contents**. Choose the **Formal** style of TOC.

Preview the file.

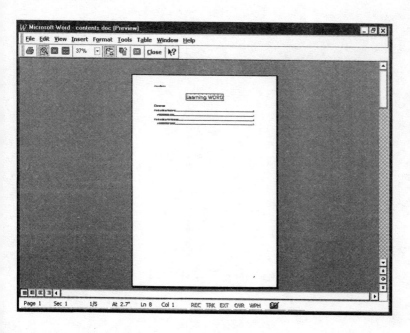

You now have a simple contents page, see how easy it is to produce. If you re-arrange the pages in your document, simply redo the Table of Contents.

Save the file as CONTENTS and close it.

Mailmerging

Mailmerging means to merge a list of names and addresses (data) with a (standard) letter.

Begin by creating a new file and enter your address and insert the date (right aligned) at the top.

Pull down the **Tools** menu and select **Mail Merge**. You will see a dialog box, click on **Create**.

Now select the following commands (in sequence).

Form Letters
Active Window
Get Data
Create Data Source

You will see the following dialog box.

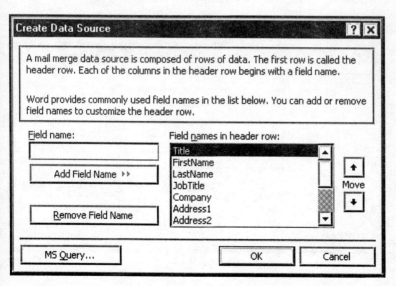

Click on **Remove Field Name** (after selecting the **Field Name** you want to remove) until you only have left the following fields.

First Name
Last Name
Company
Address 1
Address 2
City
State
Postal Code

Finally click on the **OK** button.

You will be prompted to save the file, call it MERGE.

Next click on the **Edit Data Source** and enter the following data into the **Data Form** that appears (illustrated below). Use the **Tab** key to move onto the next line.

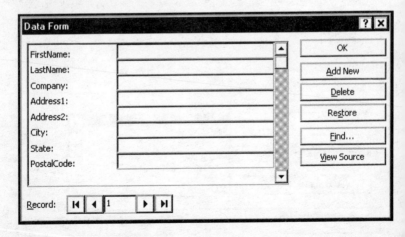

joe
smith
smith hydraulic pumps plc
the old smithy
new town industrial park
somerton
somerset
ta21 6tr

Click on the **Add New** button to enter the next record and on the **OK** button when finished.

sally
jukins
happy holidays
34 high street
(blank line)
oldtown
dorset
bh3 6tr

Then enter the fields into the letter by clicking on the **Insert Merge Field** button, **Return**ing to create a new line.

Insert Merge Field ▾

You should see a letter similar to this.

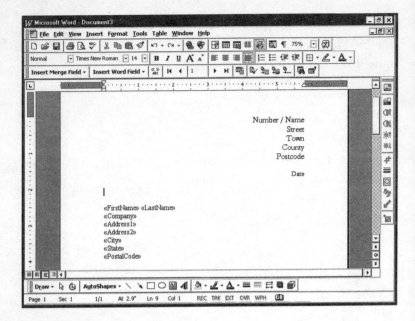

Save the file as MERGEDATA.

To merge the data with the letter, click on the **Mail Merge** button on the toolbar.

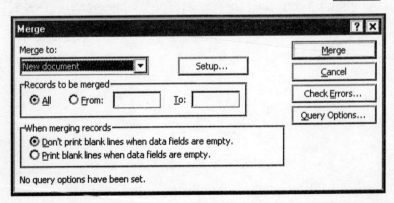

Click on **Merge** and the data should be merged to a new
document (below).

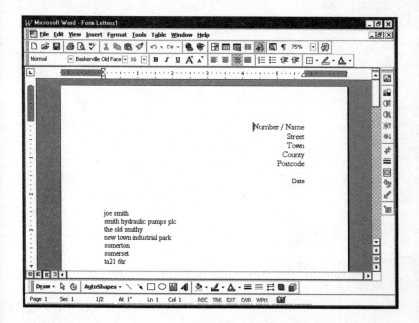

Preview the file and you should see each address appear in
sequence.

Save the file as LETTERS and close all the files.

Excel

Starting off

The Excel screen (shown below) is divided into rows (across) and columns (down). Rows are numbered and columns are lettered.

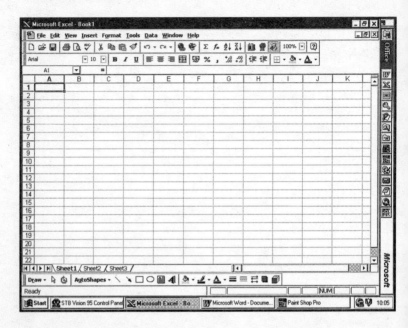

The screen is divided by gridlines into cells, each cell having a unique address, e.g. A1 or C9.

The following can be entered into cells.

☐ Text (words)
☐ Numbers
☐ Formulae (calculations)
☐ Graphics
☐ Objects (Word Art, Equations, etc.)

Moving around the worksheet

You can move around by using the cursor keys or by clicking the mouse in a cell.

Entering text or numbers

Move to the cell into which you want to enter text or numbers and type the text or number.

Then either hit the **Return** key or use the cursor keys to move the cursor to the next cell.

Enter the data (shown below) into the worksheet (the cells are shown for reference).

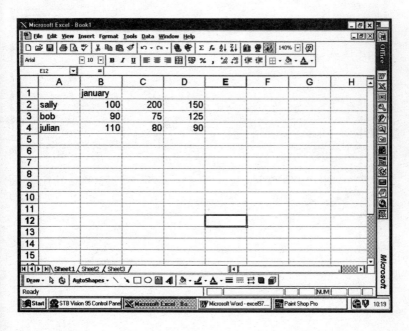

Saving your work

It is vital to save your work regularly (computers can malfunction).

Click on the **Save** button on the toolbar and save the file (call it PRAC1) to the folder you want to (it is much better to save to a hard disc rather than a floppy disc as the process is faster and more reliable).

The **Save** (**As**) screen is shown for reference.

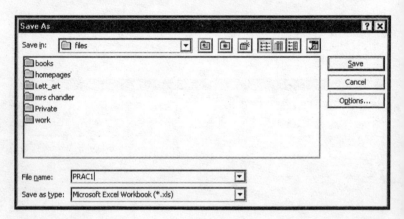

So far you have entered text, numbers and saved the file. Now to build up a more interesting and better-looking worksheet.

Copying cells

One of the advantages of a spreadsheet (over paper) is that you can copy data and formulae quickly and easily.

Click the mouse in cell **B1** and move the mouse pointer to the bottom right corner of the cell until it becomes a thin cross shape (called a fill handle).

Now click and drag the cross shape to cell **D1** and then let go of the mouse button. You will see that the program has inserted the correct months into the cells.

Aligning cells

To alter the formatting of cells, you need to highlight the cells.

To do this, click the mouse in the initial cell and drag the (large cross) so that all the cells you want to format are highlighted (the initial cell will be included but not highlighted).

Highlight cells **B1** to **D1**

Click the **Align Right** button on the toolbar.

The headings will now line up with the numbers - numbers should always be right aligned so the hundreds, tens and units are underneath each other - remember your schooldays.

Now add the words (shown below) in the appropriate cells.

A5	Total
E1	Total

Right align cell **E1**.

Your worksheet should now look like this.

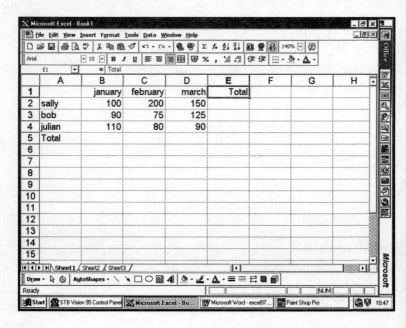

Entering formulae

It is important to understand the need to enter a calculation (rather than the answer) into the appropriate cells. If you enter a formula and then alter any of the original data, the calculation will show the change.

Click the mouse in cell **B5** and then click on the **AutoSum** button on the toolbar.

You should see the following formula entered in the cell.

	A	B	C	D	E
1		january	february	march	Total
2	sally	100	200	150	
3	bob	90	75	125	
4	julian	110	80	90	
5	Total	=SUM(B2:B4)			

Hit the **Return** key and the answer will appear.

Now copy the formula in cell **B5** across to cells **C5** to **D5** (in the same way you copied the months earlier).

Click in cell **E2** and use the **AutoSum** button to calculate the total for Sally.

Now copy the formula in **E2** to cells **E3** to **E5**.

Save your file (as PRAC1) using the **Save** button.

It should look like this.

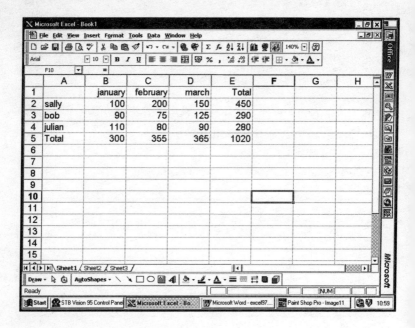

Inserting rows and columns

To insert a blank row or column click the cursor in the cell **after** the position you want to insert a row or column and then pull down the **Insert** menu and select **Rows** or **Columns**.

Click the cursor in cell **A1** and insert a row.

Enter the following text in cell **A1**.

Direct Sales Co.

Centring text (across columns)

Highlight the cells **A1** to **E1**. Then click on the
Merge and Center button on the toolbar. The
title should now be centred across the columns.

Altering the fonts

Click in cell **A1** and using the **Font Size** button, alter the
font size to 14 (point).

Then use the **Font** button to alter the font to **Times New
Roman**.

Finally, use the **Font Color** button to alter
the colour to **Red** (click on the arrow to the
right to display the colours).

To practise, alter the fonts of the months and the people's
names to whatever font, size and colour you choose (try to
be sensible).

If you pull down the **Format** menu, select **Cells** and then
Font, you have even more variety in the look of the type.

Borders and patterns

To make data stand out, you can alter the font, size and colour. Another method is to use borders and patterns.

To try this, highlight cells **A6** to **E6**, then pull down the **Format** menu, and select **Cells** followed by **Border**.

You should see the following dialog box.

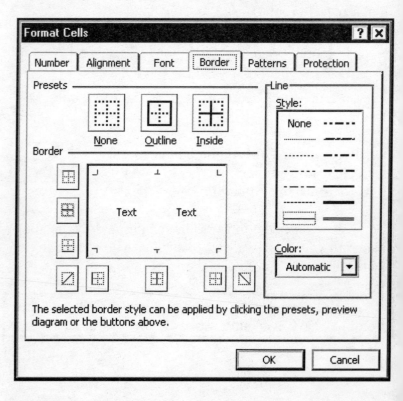

Choose the **(Line) Style**, **Color** and then click on the **Outline** button (you must click the **Outline** button last). Finally, click on **OK**.

Your cells should now have a border (you may need to click the mouse away to see the border).

If you wish, you can add shading or patterns by the same method (only choosing **Patterns** rather than **Border**).

Place a border around the months and **Save** the results. The worksheet may look similar to this.

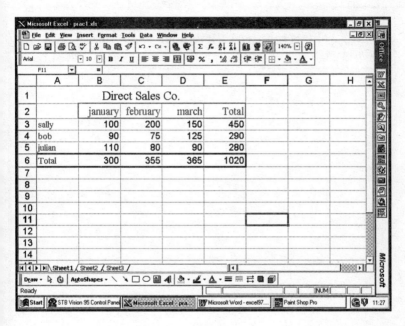

Viewing the formula

It is useful to be able to see the formula you have used. To do this hold down the **Ctrl** key and then press the key above the **Tab** key (to the left of the **1** key).

This should display the formula (repeat this to return to the figures).

If this does not work then pull down the **Tools** menu, followed by **Options**, **View** and then make sure the **Formulas** box has a tick in it (to reverse remove the tick).

Page Setup

At this stage (before printing the worksheet), it is worthwhile exploring the various layout options.

Pull down the **File** menu and then select **Page Setup**. You will see the following screen.

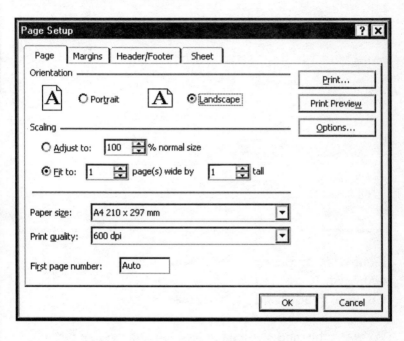

You may want to select **Landscape** and **Fit to** (one page) from this screen (to select the items, ensure a dot is shown by each - as you can see in the example).

Next select **Margins** and tick the **Center on page** boxes at the bottom (as shown in the example below).

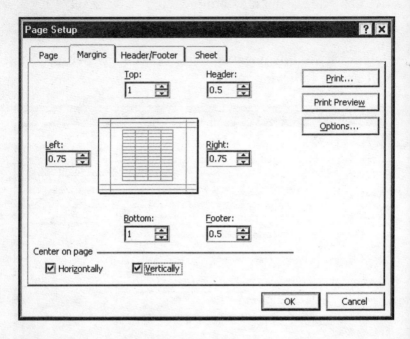

Finally select **Header/Footer** and you will be able to add your own headers and footers to the worksheet. Click on **Custom Header** and enter the data.

To insert the date or filename use the appropriate button.

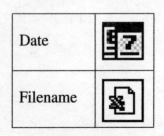

The example shows three headers, my name, the filename and the date. Footers work in a similar way.

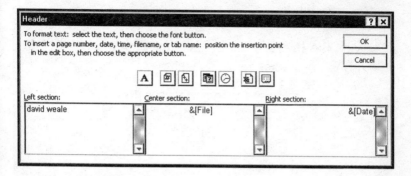

Using headers and footers is important as they allow you to identify the printout far more easily.

Add your name, the filename and the date as a header, return to the worksheet.

Previewing the worksheet

To save paper and time it is best to preview the worksheet before printing it.

Click on the **Preview** button and you should see the following screen.

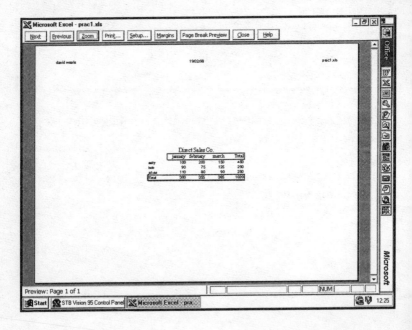

Click on the **Close** button to return to the worksheet.

Printing your worksheet

To print the worksheet, click on the **Print** button on the toolbar (if you want to have more choices, pull down the **File** menu and select **Print**). To practice, print the worksheet and then the formulae (separately).

Closing the file

Save the file, then pull down the **File** menu, and select **Close**.

To start a new file

Click on the **New** button on the toolbar and a new worksheet will appear.

A new exercise

Please enter the new worksheet.

	A	B	C	D
1	SALES FIGURES			
2	Salesperson	Year ended	Year ended	Difference
3		31-Dec-98	31-Dec-97	
4	Smith.C	24000	26000	
5	Jules.B	46000	45000	
6	Norris.T	85000	82000	
7	Torr.M	66000	99000	
8	Bates.N	35000	32000	
9	TOTALS			

Altering column (or row) width

If you enter too much text to fit in the cell, or if you alter the font size, then all the data may not fit into the cell.

With numbers, you may see the following symbol. This symbol shows that the column is not wide enough to display the numbers correctly.

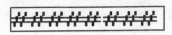

To alter the width manually, move the mouse pointer to the divide between two column letters when it will become a two-arrowhead cross.

Click and drag the divider until you are happy.

You can also alter the width by highlighting the column(s) and pulling down the **Format** menu and selecting **Column** and then **Width**.

Save the file as PRAC2.

Entering formulae

You have already used the **AutoSum** button, however you may want to enter other formulae.

In this case you are going to calculate the difference in sales between the years (the figures represent pounds).

To enter the formula carry out the following steps.

☐ Click in cell **D4** and then enter an = (addition) sign (all formulae begin with this sign - the **AutoSum** formula adds it automatically).

☐ Click the mouse in cell **B4**

☐ Enter a - (minus) sign

☐ Click the mouse pointer in cell **C4**

☐ Hit the **Return** key.

If you have carried out this correctly then the answer should appear in cell **D4**.

If you click back on cell **D4,** you should see the formula in the **Formula Bar** (as in the top line of the illustration below).

	A	B	C	D
1	SALES FIGURES			
2	Salesperson	Year ended	Year ended	Difference
3		31-Dec-98	31-Dec-97	
4	Smith.C	24000	26000	-2000
5	Jules.B	46000	45000	
6	Norris.T	85000	82000	
7	Torr.M	66000	99000	
8	Bates.N	35000	32000	
9	TOTALS			

☐ Copy the formula from **D4** to **D8**.

☐ Total the first column (using the **AutoSum** button).

☐ Copy the total across the columns.

☐ Add another person (after **Bates**). The name is **Harris.R** and the figures are 20800 and 19900 respectively. Calculate the difference by copying the formula from the cell above.

☐ The totals have not changed. You will need to redo the formula for the totals (if you insert a new row other than at the top or bottom of the table then the formula will automatically be recalculated).

76

Sorting the data

Highlight the data (but **only** rows **4** to **9**, you do not want to sort the headings or the totals).

Pull down the **Data** menu and select **Sort**. You will see the following dialog box.

Make sure that it looks like this (**Sort by** is **Column A**) and then click on the **OK** button.

The data should be sorted and look like this.

	A	B	C	D
1	SALES FIGURES			
2	Salesperson	Year ended	Year ended	Difference
3		31-Dec-98	31-Dec-97	
4	Bates.N	35000	32000	3000
5	Harris.R	20800	19900	900
6	Jules.B	46000	45000	1000
7	Norris.T	85000	82000	3000
8	Smith.C	24000	26000	-2000
9	Torr.M	66000	99000	-33000
10	TOTALS	276800	303900	-27100

Now format the worksheet in the following ways.

- ☐ Centre the title across the columns.
- ☐ Alter the fonts (size, type and colour) and add borders/shading as required (be sensible!).
- ☐ Align column headings (the columns with numbers) to the right.
- ☐ Landscape orientation.
- ☐ Fit to one page.
- ☐ Centre horizontally and vertically on the page.
- ☐ Header (your name) and footers (date and filename).
- ☐ Preview both the figures **and** the formulae (and print if you wish to).

The result may look like this (figures first, then formulae).

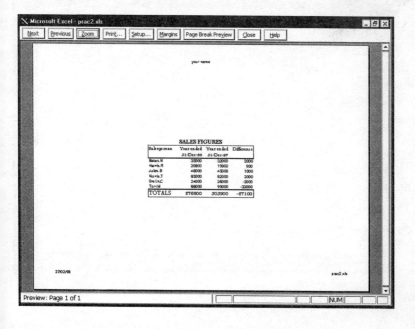

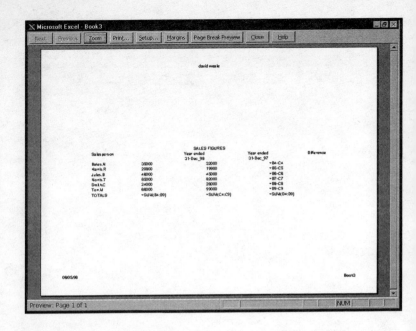

Save the file as PRAC2.

AutoFormat

A quick way of formatting a worksheet is to highlight all the data you want to format and then pulling down the **Format** menu and selecting **AutoFormat**.

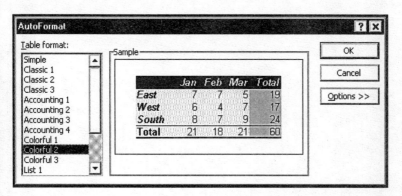

You can choose from a variety of different formats, which once applied to your worksheet can be altered, as you wish.

Normally, if you want to apply the **AutoFormat** then do so **before** any other formatting since the **AutoFormat** will overwrite some of the changes you make before you apply it.

Apply one of the **AutoFormats** to your file.

It may look similar to this when previewed.

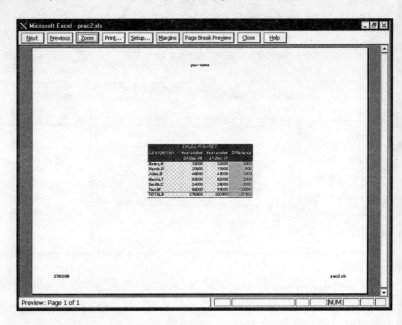

Pull down the **File** menu and select **Save As** so you can alter the file name, save your revised version as PRAC3 and close it.

Another new exercise

Enter a new worksheet (adjusting the column widths as necessary).

Prac 3

	A	B	C	D	E
1	Perfect Pets Store				
2		Original Price	Percentage Reduction	Discount	Sale Price
3	Cats	3.5	30		
4	Dogs	5.99	35		
5	Fish	9.99	25		
6	Guinea Pigs	4.99	10		
7	Totals				

82

Arithmetic calculations

The symbols used for arithmetic operators are as follows:

Addition	+
Subtraction	-
Multiply	*
Division	/

☐ Remember that **all** formulae have to begin with the = sign

☐ Now calculate the **Discount** Column by working out the percentages (**Original Price** times **Percentage Reduction**) - use the % key for the percentage. You can see the formula in the illustration.

	A	B	C	D	E
1	Perfect Pets Store				
2		Original Price	Percentage Reduction	Discount	Sale Price
3	Cats	3.5	30	=B3*C3%	
4	Dogs	5.99	35		
5	Fish	9.99	25		
6	Guinea Pigs	4.99	10		
7	Totals	24.47	100		

☐ Calculate the **Sale Price** column (**Original Price** minus **Discount**).

☐ Copy these down to the other rows and total the columns.

At this stage, your worksheet should correspond closely to this.

	A	B	C	D	E
1	Perfect Pets Store				
2		Original Price	Percentage Reduction	Discount	Sale Price
3	Cats	3.5	30	1.05	2.45
4	Dogs	5.99	35	2.0965	3.8935
5	Fish	9.99	25	2.4975	7.4925
6	Guinea Pigs	4.99	10	0.499	4.491
7	Totals	24.47	100	6.143	18.327

Formatting numbered cells

As you can see the number of decimal places varies from cell to cell. This is poor layout and makes the figures difficult to read. You should be consistent with the number of decimal places within a column.

Highlight all the numbered cells and pull down the **Format** menu, choose **Cells**, and then **Number**. From the list select **Currency** and then **2** decimal places (this should be the default).

All your numbers should now have pound signs in front and have two decimal places.

Obviously, this is incorrect for the **Percentage Reduction** column, so format this to **Number** (zero decimal places).

Cell alignment

You can make the layout more attractive by altering the alignment of cells. In this example, the column headings are too wide.

Highlight cells **B2** to **E2** and **Format**, **Column** and **Width** (to 10). With the cells **B2** to **E2** still highlighted, **Format**, **Row** and **Height** (to 25).

Highlight cells **B2** to **E2**, pull down the **Format** menu, and select **Cells** and then **Alignment**.

Alter the settings to those shown on the next page, the text will wrap around and the worksheet will look more sensibly laid out.

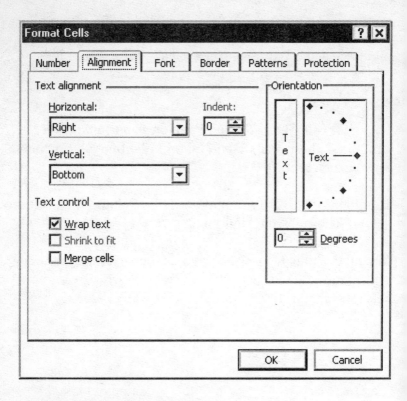

Use the following formatting.

☐ Landscape orientation.
☐ Fit to one page.
☐ Centre horizontally and vertically on the page.
☐ Header (your name) and footers (date and filename).
☐ Centre the business name across the columns.
☐ Alter the fonts (size, type and colour) and add borders/shading as required (be sensible!).
☐ Preview both the figures **and** the formulae (and print if you wish to).
☐ Save the file as PRAC4.

The result (when previewed) could look similar to this.

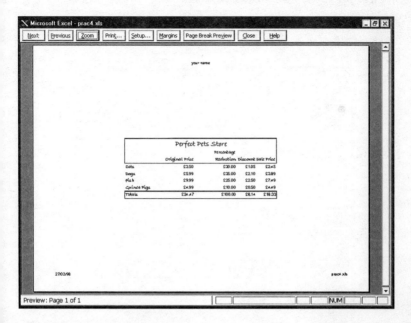

Close the file.

The next exercise

Enter the data shown below into a new worksheet, adjusting column width as necessary.

	A	B	C	D
1	Personal Expenditure Analysis (£)			
2	Item	Jan		
3	Mortgage	50.5	52	41.2
4	Electricity	3.5	5.2	12.67
5	Rates	7.6	7.6	7.6
6	Food	41.26	45.4	39.3
7	Motor	9.9	10.89	10.5
8	Holidays	3.5	3.5	3.5
9	Insurance	3.9	3.9	3.9
10	Fun	11.1	12.21	11.45
11	Savings	20	20	20
12	Total			
13	Income	155	155	155
14	Excess			

☐ Copy the month across to the other columns.
☐ Total the expenditure for Jan and copy this across
☐ Calculate the **Excess** for each month (**Income** minus **Total**).
☐ Save the file as PRAC5.

Functions

You have already used the **SUM** function, here are some more functions which you can enter manually.

Add these column headings to your worksheet (columns **E** to **H**).

	A	B	C	D	E	F	G	H
1	Personal Expenditure Analysis (£)							
2	Item	Jan	Feb	Mar	Total	Minimum	Maximum	Average

Use the **AutoSum** to calculate the first total (cell **E3**).

In the **Minimum** column (cell **F3**) enter the following formula (do not type in the cell references, but click the mouse in the first cell and drag to include all the cells you want - this works the same as typing in the cell references but is more accurate and quicker).

=MIN(B3:D3)

Do the same for **G3** and **H3**, substituting **MAX** and **AVERAGE** respectively in place of the word **MIN**.

Highlight cells **E3** to **H3** and copy them down (together).

Now format the worksheet to:

☐ Format the figures to two decimal places (but no pound sign) - use **Format**, **Cells**, **Number** and **Number** (again).
☐ Alter the fonts (size, type and colour) and add borders/shading as required - you may want to use **AutoFormat**.
☐ Centre the title across the columns.
☐ Align column headings (the columns with numbers) to the right and alter the column widths as desired.
☐ Landscape orientation.
☐ Fit to one page.
☐ Centre horizontally and vertically on the page.
☐ Include a header (your name) and footers (date and filename).
☐ Preview both the figures and the formulae (and print if you wish to).

It could look similar to this when previewed.

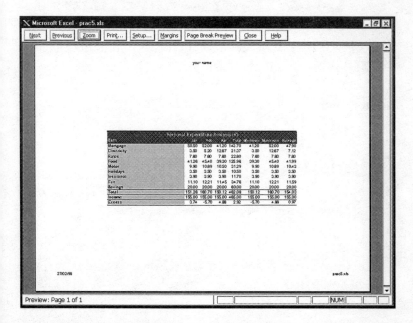

Save and close the file.

Charts and Graphs

One of the best ways of communicating numerical data is in the form of a chart. Many people find numbers a little frightening but can assimilate quite complex numerical information if it is visual in nature.

The Chart Wizard

Open the file called PRAC1 and highlight all the data (except the bottom total row) - (i.e. highlight cells **A1** to **E5**).

Click the mouse pointer on the **Chart Wizard** button on the toolbar to begin the process.

You will be presented with a series of dialog boxes into which you enter data or instructions. Enter these as shown in the illustrations below.

The first of these lets you select the chart type you want. In this case, the **Column** is a good choice.

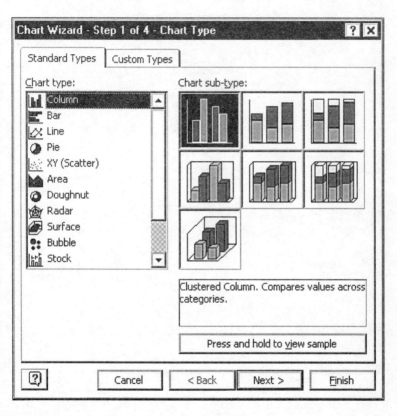

Be careful to choose chart types that show your data to best advantage i.e. communicate it clearly.

The next screen allows you to alter the way in which the series are shown, you can choose either **Rows** or **Columns**.

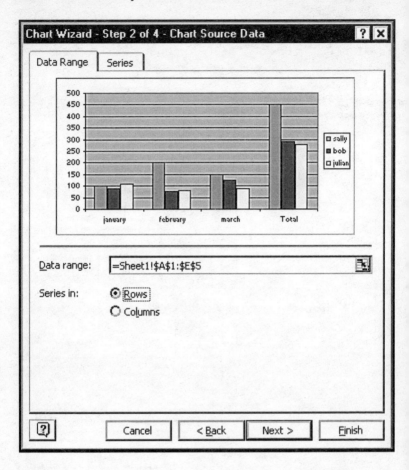

You can select either **Rows** or **Columns**, choose the one that shows the data in the most effective way.

Here you enter the **Chart title** and the **X** and **Y** axis labels.

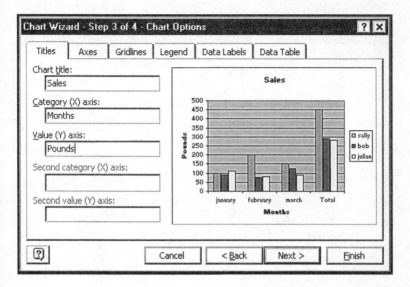

The final screen gives you two choices, I suggest **very strongly** that you select **As new sheet**. This will give you far more control and flexibility over your chart.

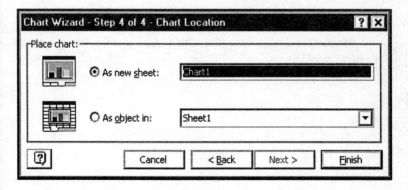

Assuming your have made the same choices, your chart will look like this.

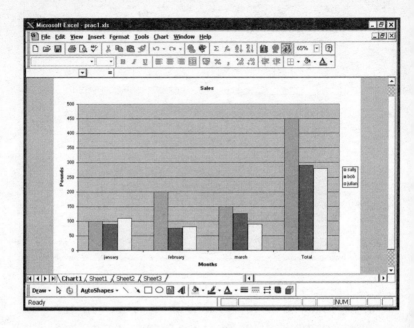

Altering the look of the chart

The simplest way to alter the chart is to click on the **Chart Wizard** and alter the **Chart type**. You can make alterations to the choices you originally made and produce a different chart.

If you ever want to create two different charts from the same data, it is best to use the **Edit** menu followed by **Move or Copy Sheet** to create a copy which contains all the data, formatting, headers and footers and so on and then alter the copy.

The dialog box is shown for reference, note that you should ensure that the **Create a copy** box is ticked.

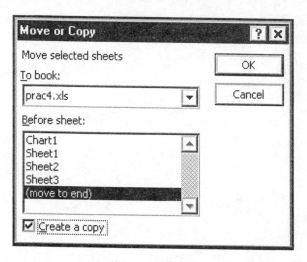

Altering the text font & alignment

You can select any text within the chart by double-clicking it and a dialog box will be displayed allowing you to make changes to the look of the text.

For example, if you double click the title, you will see the following dialog box, which has three sections

I suggest you experiment with each of these (remember to use the **Undo** button on the toolbar if you make a mess)	

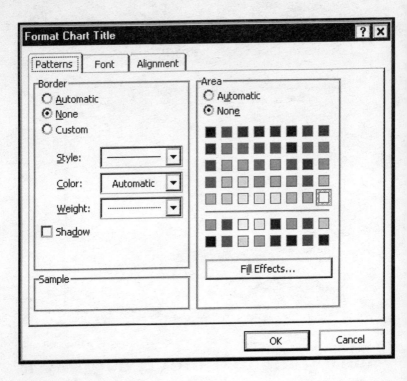

In **Patterns** you can add a **Border** and/or alter the **Chart Title** area.

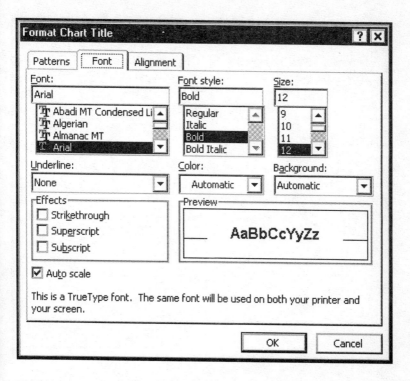

Font enables you to change the font type, size and colour.

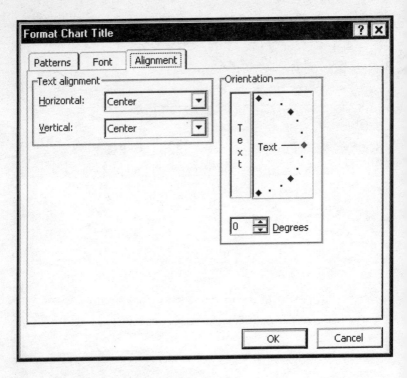

In **Alignment** you can alter the **Orientation** (by dragging the **Text** line) and **Alignment**.

Altering the chart

Similarly you can double-click any part of the chart and alter how it looks using the dialog boxes that appear.

For example, if you double-click any of the columns in the chart you will see this dialog box.

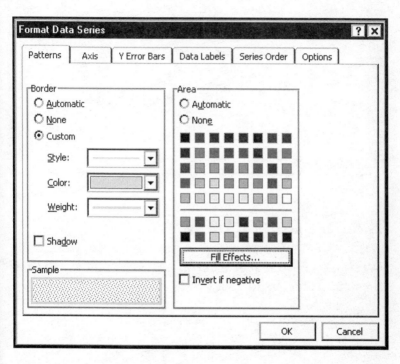

By selecting **Custom Border** and then **Fill Effects (Area),** you can alter the look of the column.

I have made various changes to the original chart, see what you can do.

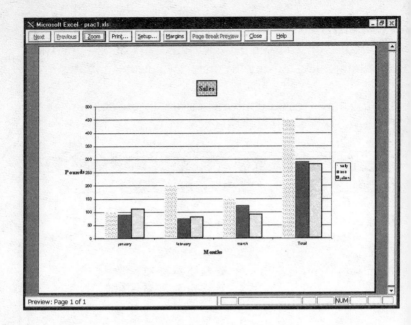

Headers & Footers

These work in exactly the same way as in worksheets (**View** menu). Add your name as a header and the date and filename as footers to your chart.

Changing the names of the worksheets

Now you have more than one worksheet in the file, it is useful to make the names of the worksheets meaningful.

Double-click the name (i.e. **Sheet 1**) along the bottom of the screen and type in **Direct sales spreadsheet**. Do the same for the chart calling it **Direct sales chart**.

| ◄ | ◄ | ► | ►| \ **Direct sales chart** / Direct sales spreadsheet /

Save and close the file.

Adding legends and X-series labels

Often you will be charting a worksheet where the data does not allow you to easily include the legends or X-series labels (e.g. the column headings may be on two rows as in this example or the X-series labels may not be included when you highlight the data.

Open the file PRAC2 and create a column chart using the data in cells **B4** to **D9** (ignoring the title, column headings and totals for now).

Start the **Chart Wizard** and select **Column** chart type. On the second screen click on the **Series** button and you will see the following.

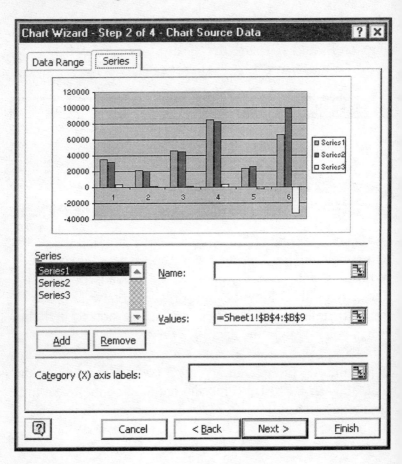

At present, there are no X-series labels (along the X-axis) and the legend is not very helpful.

Changing the X-series labels

Click on the button (at the end of the **Category X axis labels** box).

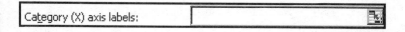

This will return you to the worksheet, highlight the names of the people and then click on the (end) button of the dialog box to return to the chart.

You will see the X-series labels appear in the chart.

Changing the legend descriptions

Highlight each series (Series1, etc.) in turn and type the correct description in the **Name** box.

Alternatively, you can use the technique described above. This is how the **Chart Wizard** dialog box should look at this stage.

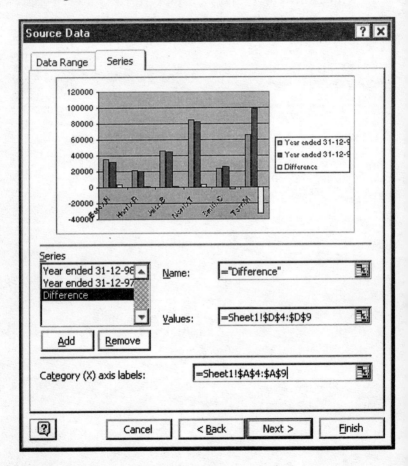

Carry on with the **Wizard** adding the necessary data.

Altering the position of the X-series labels

Click the X axis (be careful to be precise where you click) and you should see this dialog box. Make sure you are looking at the **Patterns** dialog box.

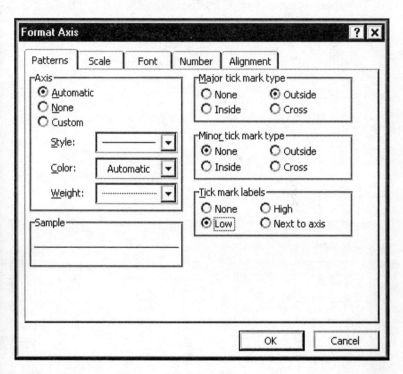

Ensure that you have selected **Low** for **Tick mark labels** and see the result. This avoids the labels getting in the way of the columns.

Apply the following formatting:

☐ Format the title to a larger size.
☐ Place a shadowed border around the whole chart (double-click the edge of the chart to display the dialog box).
☐ Alter the look of the columns so that it is easy to distinguish between them when printed in black and white.
☐ Enter your name as a header
☐ Enter the file name and date as footers

Preview the file and if it looks satisfactory, print it out.

Here is my version.

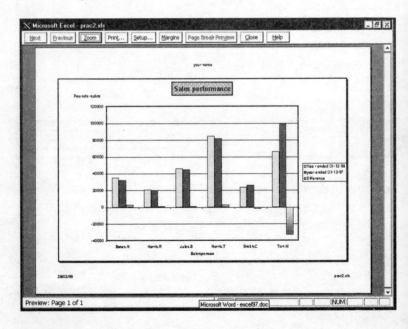

Save and close the file.

Practice

Open PRAC4 and create a column chart (excluding the **Percentage Reduction** column and the totals, but including the **Sale Price** column) i.e. include cells **A2:B6** and **D2:E6**

You can select the data you want to include by highlighting the data in the first row or column and then hold the **CTRL** key down and click and drag the mouse to highlight the remainder of the data (which need not be in consecutive rows or columns).

Use your imagination to produce a professional looking result.

Adding text boxes and arrows

You may want to add some narrative to your work.

You are going to add a text box with suitable text to show the most expensive pet. To do this, you need to use the **Drawing** toolbar (**View** menu, **Toolbars**, **Drawing**).

Click on the **Text Box** button and drag the mouse to create a text box. Enter the text you want (altering the font, resizing the box and so on as necessary).

Click on the **arrow** button to draw an arrow (if you then double-click the arrow you can alter the way it looks).

Here is an example of how the final version could look.

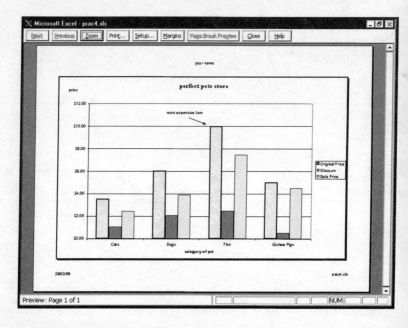

Save and close the worksheet and exit Excel.

PowerPoint

Starting off

After loading the program, you will then see the dialog box shown below.

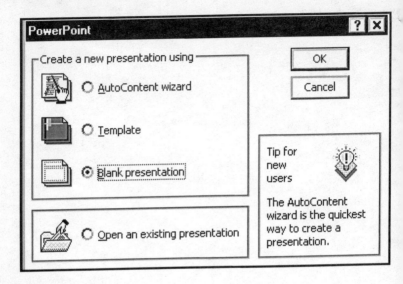

Creating a new presentation

If necessary, select **Blank Presentation** by clicking the mouse so that a dot appears in front of the words and then click on **OK**.

You should see the following:

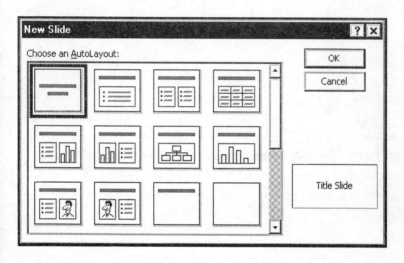

If not already selected, click on the very first **AutoLayout** and then on **OK**.

You will see the title screen.

Entering Text

Make the window full-screen by clicking on the appropriate button (if it is not already full-screen).

Enter the following title (click the mouse within the existing text to begin).

| My First Slide Show |

Enter the following sub-title:

| Using PowerPoint |

Click on the **New Slide** button (top toolbar).

Select the second **AutoLayout** and you should see the
following screen.

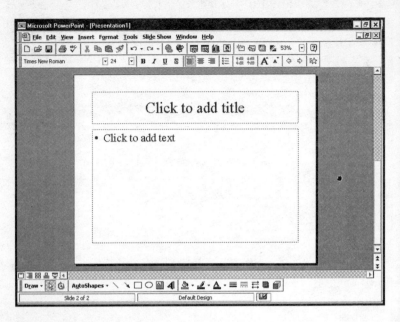

Add the following title:

The First Slide

Add the text:

Line One

Press the **Return** key and then enter the following lines, pressing **Return** between each:

```
Line Two
Line Three
Line Four
```

Click on the **New Slide** button and again choose the second layout.

Add the following title:

```
The Second Slide
```

Add the text (exactly as spelt).

```
Line Fiive
Line Siix
Line Sevenn
Line Ate
Line Nine
```

You have now created three slides.

Saving your work

It is best to save your work regularly. To do so click on the **Save** button (upper toolbar), click in the **File name** box and name your file PRESENT1. Save it to the folder of your choice.

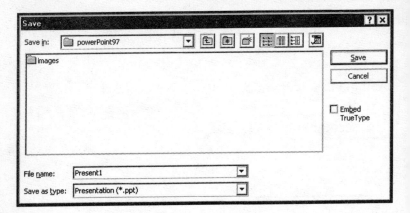

Text editing

Use the double headed arrows on the bottom right of the screen to move back to the initial slide (titled **My First Slide Show**).

To alter the font, highlight the text by clicking and dragging the mouse, then click on the arrow to the right of each of the toolbar buttons (shown below) to pull down the choices and then scroll up or down the list until you get to your choice.

Alter the title font to **Algerian 54 pt** and the subtitle to the same font and **44 pt** size.

Use the double arrow buttons to move to the next slide (titled **The First Slide**).

Now you are going to alter the size of the title (of this slide) to **Algerian 54 pt** and the text to **Times New Roman 44 pt**.

Move to the final slide and alter the fonts in the same way

Move back to the slide titled **The First Slide**.

Select the text (by highlighting) and pull down the **Format** menu and then **Line Spacing**.

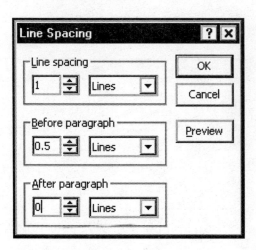

Alter the **Before Paragraph** to **0.5** and then click on the **Preview** button. If satisfactory click on **OK**.

Make sure all the text is still selected and then use the **Centre** button on the toolbar to centre the text (note that this centres each line between the margins)

Move to the final slide and again highlight the text.

From the **Format** menu select **Bullet,** selecting **Wingdings**® from the **Bullets from** list, choose a new bullet, then alter the various options (**Color**, **Size** and so on), and finally click on **OK**.

Do this again, this time choosing a sensible bullet.

You now need to use the **Drawing** toolbar, this should be displayed along the bottom of the screen, however if it is not then pull down the **View** menu, select **Toolbars** and then **Drawing**. The toolbar looks like this.

Make sure the text is still highlighted and then use the **Font Colour** button on the **Drawing** toolbar to colour the text **Blue** (you may need to click on the arrow to the right of the button and then select **More Font Colors**).

Now just highlight the word **Sevenn** and change its colour to **Black**.

Move back to the first slide (titled **My First Slide Show**) and select the subtitle by clicking to display the text border.

From the **Draw** menu (**Drawing** toolbar), choose **Rotate or Flip** and then **Free Rotate**. Grab one of the corners of the text border and rotate the text.

Alternatively, you could also use the rotate button to the right of the **Draw** menu.

Grab the text by clicking on a side of the rectangular border, then dragging it further down the slide.

Finally click on the **Spelling** button and spell check your slides, correcting as necessary.

The spelling dialog box is shown below.

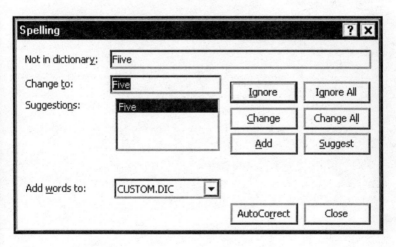

You have various options; you can **Ignore** or **Ignore All** (occurrences of the word), **Change** to the correct spelling or **Add** to the dictionary.

Remember that the spellchecker may identify a word that is correct but not within its dictionary. The spell check did not pick up the word **Ate** in the final slide. You will need to alter this manually.

Transitions

So far, you have produced a series of three slides. Now you are going to see how they look as a slide show, using the transition effect (this alters the way in which each slide is loaded onto the screen).

Click on the **Slide Sorter View** button (bottom left of the screen).

You will see all the slides together.

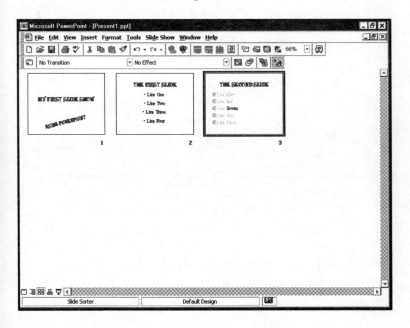

Pull down the **Edit** menu and choose **Select All**.

Use the **Slide Transition** button to create a transition, you can see the effects displayed as you choose the different transitions.

Alternatively, pull down the **Slide Show** menu and select **Slide Transition**.

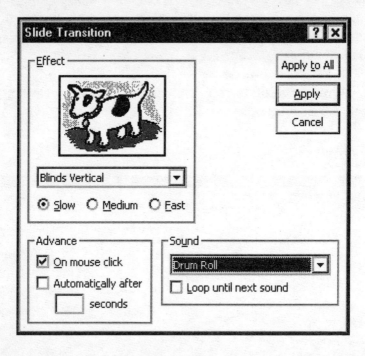

You can alter the speed of the transition and add sounds. I suggest you begin with the **Slow**.

Finally, click on the **Apply to All** button.

Animations

With all the slides selected, you can apply special effects to the way in which the lines of text are displayed. To use this click on the arrow to the right of the box (shown below) which is displayed on the toolbar to the right of the **Transitions** button.

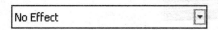

Select the animation you want to use.

Now, click on the **Slide Show** button along the bottom left of the screen and use the left-hand mouse button to advance the text and slides.

Practise altering the **Transition** and **Animations** so you can see the effect of the different techniques.

Use the **Slide View** button to return to the slides.

Looking at your Slides

Slide Sorter

You have already used this to produce transitions and animations for the slide show, another use is to rearrange the slides.

Click on the **Slide Sorter** button. You will see all the slides together. Now grab the last slide with the mouse and drag it in front of the first slide (you will see a line appear where the slide will be moved to).

Move it back.

Printing the slides

You can print your slides one to a page onto paper or you can print them onto transparencies directly using a colour ink-jet printer.

You can print the slides (up to) six to a page so you can issue them as handouts to your audience.

To print, pull down the **File** menu and select **Print** and select the options you require, the illustration shows the options for printing six to a page.

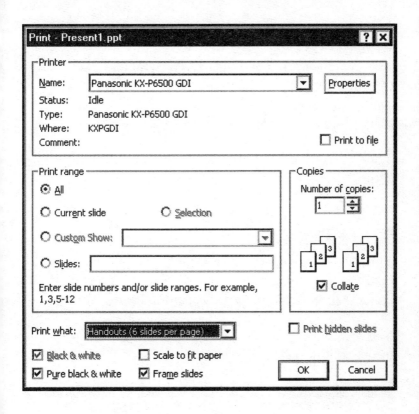

File Handling

Save the file again.

If you want to save the file under a different name or to a different directory, you need to pull down the **File** menu and then choose **Save As**.

Close the file (**File** and **Close**).

Adding Graphics

The fun starts. **Used sensibly**, graphics add to a presentation.

Start a new file (click on the **New File** button on the left of the upper toolbar). Then choose the blank **AutoLayout** (bottom right of the choices).

Slide Designs

You can add a background design to your slides (and this is normally recommended) by clicking on the A**pply Design** button (upper toolbar).

You should see a list of designs with a small illustration to the right of the selected design.

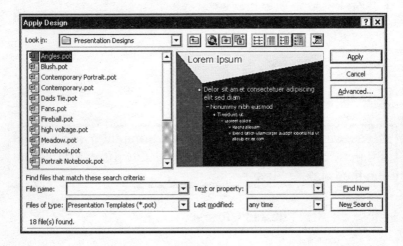

Choose the design you want to apply by scrolling down the list using the cursor keys to move down the list. Click on **Apply** to add the chosen design.

If you are to apply a design then it is best to apply it at the start of the creation of your slide show, since it may alter any existing fonts and layout.

Clipart

Then pull down the **Insert** menu, **Picture** and
then **Clip Art** (or click on the **Insert Clip Art**
button).

The Microsoft Clip Gallery will be loaded.

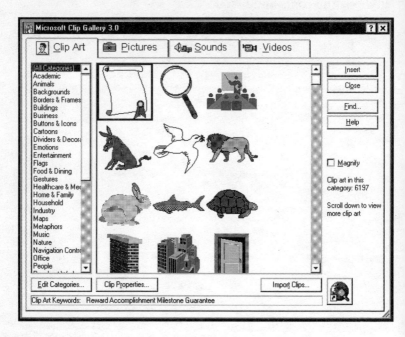

Choose the **Academic** category and from that a picture (shown below). Click on **Insert**.

The picture will appear within the slide. Do not worry about its size or position at present.

WordArt

Create a second slide (**New Slide** button) and select the blank **AutoLayout**.

Now pull down the **Insert** menu and choose **Object** and from the list **Microsoft WordArt 3**.

Enter the following text (by overtyping the original text) and after entering the text click on the **Update Display** button

> **Fancy Letters**

Experiment with each of the buttons along the upper
toolbar (these buttons appear and disappear with the **Word
Art** module) to achieve the effect you want, clicking
outside the box when finished.

Remember if you want to alter it afterwards simply double-
click the mouse on the text and **Word Art** will be loaded
automatically.

Do not worry about its size or position at present.

Your slide may look like this.

Organisation Charts

Click on the **New Slide** button and then select the **Organisation Chart** AutoLayout.

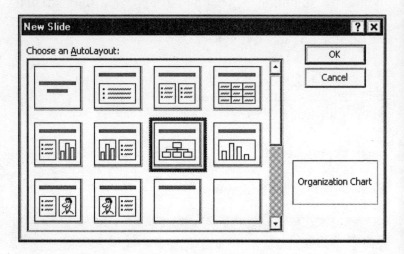

Once the slide has appeared, double click the organisation chart button and the module will (eventually) appear.

Make the window full screen.

Click on the box to the far right and delete it (use the **Delete** key).

Click on the **Subordinate** button and then on the box to the left. This will add the subordinate below that box.

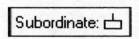

Now add a **Co-worker** box to the
side of the **Subordinate** box.

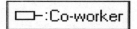

Pull down the **Edit** menu, **Select Levels**, and then **Levels 1**
to **3**.

Pull down the **Boxes** menu and select the **Color**, then
colour the boxes **white**.

In a similar way, colour the borders of the boxes **red**
(**Boxes**, **Border Color**).

Finally pull down the **Chart** menu and alter the
Background Color to **yellow**.

Add the following text by overtyping the existing text by
clicking within each box, typing and then clicking outside
each box when finished.

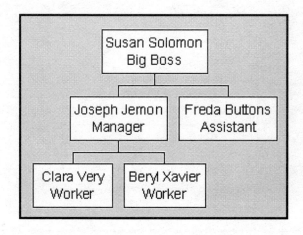

Pull down the **File** menu and then **Exit and Return** (and **Yes** to any question that appears).

If you want to make any changes, double-click the chart to load the organisation chart module.

Click in the title area and enter the title:

Swansong Company PLC

Alter the font size to 44 pt.

You have created your own customised organisation chart, do not worry about its size or position at present.

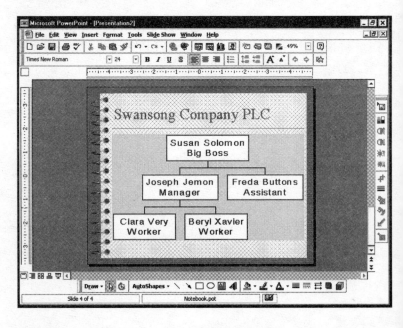

Finally, save your new file as PRESENT2.

Colouring Objects

Go to the first slide. Size the picture to **150%** (height and width) and move it into the centre of the slide (**Format**, **Picture** & **Size**).

Making sure the picture is selected, which should automatically display the **Picture** toolbar. If it does not then using the **View** menu, select **Toolbars**.

Use the **Recolor Picture** button to bring up the dialog box and then alter the colours of the image.

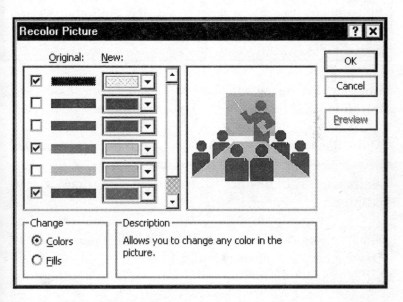

You can see the changes as you make them and save the file.

Please note that this may not work if you ungroup objects.

Grouping/Ungrouping

Now select the image and using the **Draw** menu (**Drawing** toolbar) select **Ungroup**. The picture will be ungrouped into its components and each of these can be manipulated separately (answer **Yes** to the question which appears).

If you want to further ungroup elements of the picture, click on the individual element and ungroup it.

If the image reverts to its original colours (which may happen where images have been ungrouped) then you can readjust the colours by clicking on the part of the (ungrouped) image you want to recolor, pulling down the **Format** menu and selecting **Colors and Lines** and then alter the **Fill**.

Click off the image and then grab each of the students at the far left and far right and delete them one at a time.

Move the teacher away from the board and then **Insert** a new image of a donkey (**Insert**, **Picture**, **Clip Art**, **Animals**). Size this to fit the board and drag it into position.

Finally using the **Edit** menu, **Select All** then pull down the **Draw** menu, and choose **Group**.

The result could look like this.

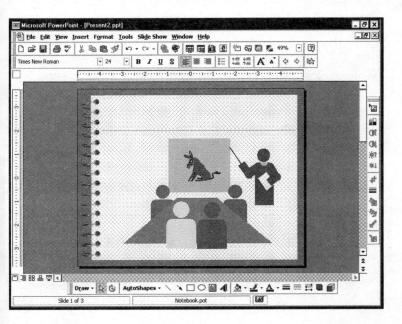

Save the file.

Rotate/Flip

This has already been looked at with respect to text.

Select the image, scale to (say) **30%** (**Format, Object, Size**), making sure the **Lock aspect ratio** box is ticked.

Click on the **Copy** button and then on the **Paste** button **three** times. You should now have four images.

Grab each, move it away from the others, and then use the **Draw** menu and **Rotate/Flip** to arrange them.

> You may need to **ungroup** each image, **rotate** it and then **group** it again.

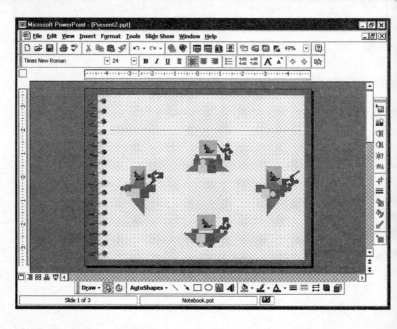

Save the file.

Borders/Arrows

Go to the last slide containing the organisation chart. Scale the chart to (say) 50%

Use the **Insert Clip Art** button to insert a picture, choose a suitable image for Susan.

Scale this to a suitable size and move it to the right of the box for Susan Soloman.

Using the **Draw** menu, click on the rectangle shape button and draw a rectangle around the picture of Susan.

If the image is now lost behind the rectangle, simply click on **Draw** and then **Order** and finally **Send Backward** (this sends the rectangle behind the original picture, bringing the picture to the front). You can alter the colour of the rectangle using the **Format**, **Colors and Lines** and **Fill Color**.

Now click on the **Arrow** button and draw an arrow from the picture to Susan.

With the arrow selected, pull down the **Format** menu and then **Colors and Lines** and alter the line colour and style of the arrow (or you can double click the arrow).

Now add a picture and arrow for Joseph (the manager).

The result may look similar to this.

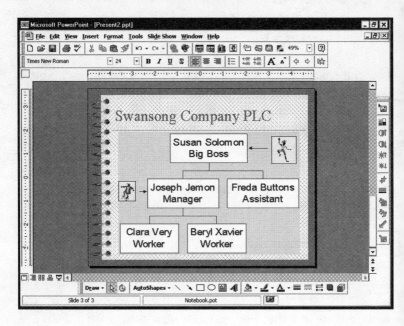

Finally, save the file.

Adding sounds (and movies)

You can add sounds and movies to your slides, though this can make the slide show slower to display.

Move back to the very first slide, move the pictures into the bottom two-thirds of the slide.

Pull down the **Format** menu and **Slide Layout**. Select the second to last **AutoLayout** (this should just impose a title area on to the slide).

Add the following title:

Sounds and movies too!

Pull down the **Insert** menu and then **Movies and Sounds** followed by **Sounds from File**. Select a sound, it will appear within the slide as a speaker icon.

I have enlarged it in the illustration below so you can see it clearly.

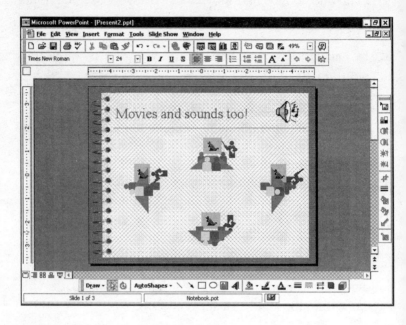

When you run your slide show you can click the icon with the mouse and you will hear the sound.

Pull down the **Slide Show** menu, then **Custom Animation**, followed by **Timing**. Select the **Media** (item) and then select **Play Settings** and finally **More options**. If you click the **Loop until stopped** choice then the music will keep playing until you click the right hand mouse button.

Movies work in a similar way.

Save and close the file.

Altering Slides

Making changes on the master slide will affect all the slides making up the presentation.

Open the first file you created (PRESENT1), using the **Open** button to do so.

Master Slides

Click on the **View** menu and then **Master** and finally **Slide Master**. The master will appear.

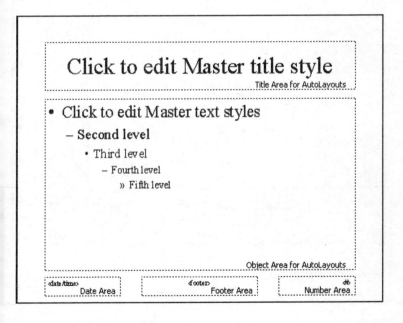

Anything you add to the master slide will appear on every slide in the slide show.

Highlight the *<date/time>* and pull down the **Insert** menu and select **Date and Time**, choose one of these.

Highlight the *<footer>* and enter your name.

Return to the slides by clicking on the **Slide View** button and go to the initial slide. Now click on the **Slide Show** button to display your slides with the time/date and your name shown on each.

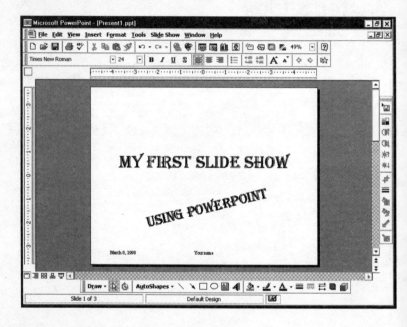

Save and close the file.

Access

What is a database

Databases are used to store information, for example customer or employee names and details. The data can be looked at (interrogated) in different ways, e.g. all the customers within a postal area could be printed out. The data can be added to, edited, deleted and viewed in various ways (forms, reports, etc).

The structure

A datafile is made up of records, there being as many records as there are items in the database (e.g. every employee would have their own record within the database).

A record is made up of fields; a field has two parts, the field name and the data in that field. Each record will comprise several fields, each containing a different type of data.

field	data
Surname	Adams
Christian name	Sarah
D.O.B.	01/6/54
Email	Saraha@cara.net

An individual record

Database programs are available in different levels of complexity and sophistication.

Flat-form databases

These are similar to the traditional card index file. The ways in which data can be looked at varies with the sophistication of the program (and of the user). Usually you can look at the data using multiple fields (e.g. all those employees aged over 50 earning more than £15000); the data can be sorted into any order. It can be printed or displayed on the screen. Other facilities include being able to check data as it is entered, and customised screen designs for data input.

Relational databases

These are a more complex version of a database. More than one database file can be opened at one time and the files can be manipulated together.

For example, for security purposes, a firm may decide to have two datafiles for the employees, one a personnel file (each record containing names, ages, home address, etc.) and the other a salary file (each record containing names and salary details).

These operate as separate datafiles, but in a relational structure they can be linked (if needed) by a common field e.g. the name field.

Thus an authorised person could look at both datafiles together and would be able to look at both salary details and personnel data (something other employees could not do), and could manipulate data across both files, e.g. add new data, create new fields, etc., which would update both databases.

Beginnings

When you start up Access, you will see the following screen.

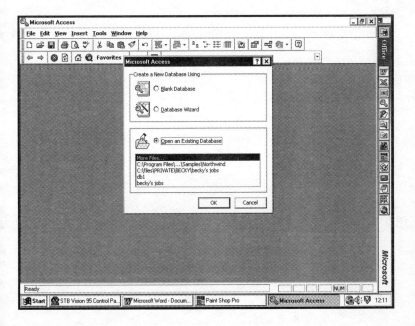

Choose **Database Wizard**.

On the following screen, click the **Database** tab.

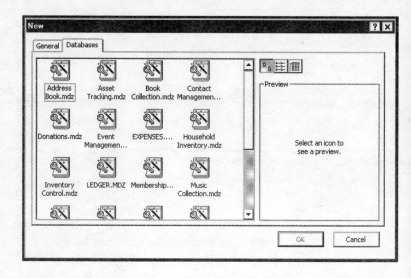

From this screen (note the buttons on the right which let you look at the files in different ways), choose **Address Book**.

Next, you will be asked to save the file.

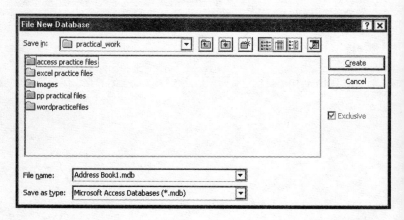

Accept the file name but be careful to select the folder you want to save it in.

Follow through the **Wizard**, choosing the options described below (if no option is mentioned, just accept the screen and move onto the next).

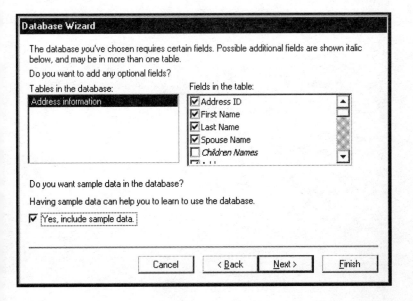

On the screen above, ensure that there is a tick by the **Yes, include sample data** box.

Work through the remainder of the screens, choosing the **screen display** and the **style** you want, but otherwise accepting the default settings.

You should now see the **Main Switchboard** (this is automatically created by the **Wizard** and enables you to carry out various tasks with your database).

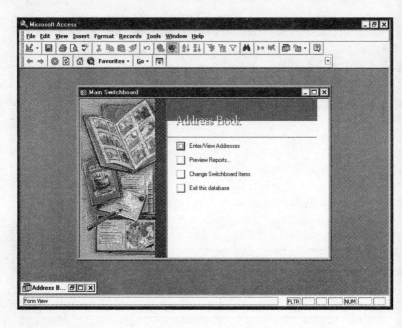

Note that the actual database in minimised in the bottom left-hand corner.

Editing the data

Click on the **Enter/View Addresses** button and the data entry form will be shown.

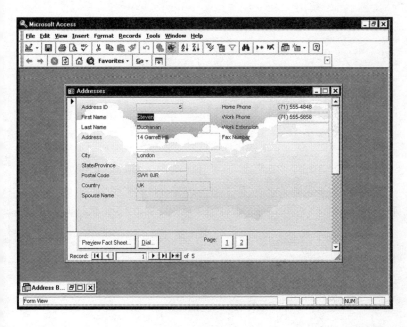

Adding records

Click on the button (bottom of the window) to add a new records and enter the following data (you will need to click on the **Page 2** button to enter the final lines of data).

First Name	Jeremiah
Last Name	Puddleduck
Address	24 Mill Lane
City	Sunbottom
State/Province	Somerset
Postal Code	BA45 5RT
Country	UK
Spouse Name	Maria
Home Phone	(0197) 54326754
Work Phone	(0197) 34433662
Work Extension	345
Fax Number	(0197) 36645980
Email Address	jerpud@virgin.net
Birthdate	10/07/54

Now enter this record by clicking on the **New Record** button.

First Name	Sally
Last Name	Jones
Address	Hilltop
City	East Millbrook
State/Province	Somerset
Postal Code	TA34 7UT
Country	UK
Spouse Name	Frederick
Home Phone	(0189) 73453349
Work Phone	(0156) 23765454
Work Extension	56
Email Address	sallyj@net.com
Birthdate	05/08/33

You should now have seven records in your database.

Return to the **Switchboard** by closing down the **Addresses** window.

Previewing reports

Click on the **Preview Reports** button to see this screen.

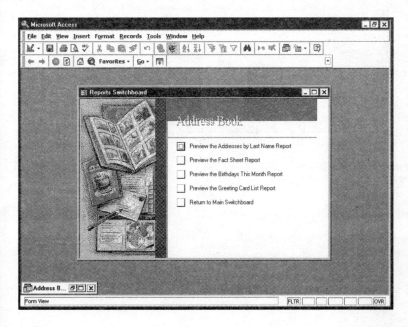

You can look at your database report in various ways, for example **Preview the Addresses by Last Name Report**.

Addresses by Last Name

Name	Address	City	State/Prov.	Postal Code	Country	Home Phone
B						
Buchanan, Steven	14 Garrett Hill	London		SW1 8JR	UK	(71) 555-4848
D						
Dwosko, Nancy	507 - 20th Ave. E. Apt. 2A	Seattle	WA	98122	USA	(306) 555-9857
F						
Fuller, Andrew	908 W. Capital Way	Tacoma	WA	98401	USA	(306) 555-9482
J						
Jones, Sally	Hilltop	East Millwork	Somerset	TA34 7UP	UK	(0129) 7345694-2
L						
Lanaring, Janet	722 Moss Bay Blvd.	Kirkland	WA	98033	USA	(306) 555-9412
P						
Peacock, Margaret	4110 Old Redmond Rd.	Redmond	WA	98052	USA	(306) 555-8122
Puddleduck, Jeremiah	24 Mill Lane	Suntellam	Somerset	BA455RT	UK	(0197) 545087754

01 April 1998

Page 1 of 1

Alternatively, **Preview the Fact Sheet Report**.

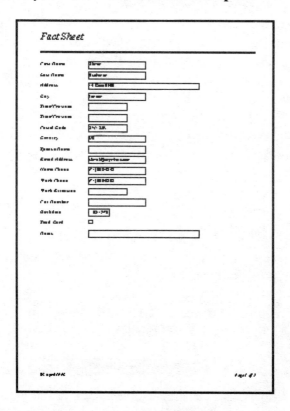

Now select **Return to Main Switchboard**.

Finally, click on **Exit this Database**.

Blank databases

The **Wizards** are useful if you are creating a standard type of database or are a beginner or want to create something quickly. For some applications, the Wizards are excellent, e.g. Students and Classes contains a sophisticated structure.

Any database you create using a Wizard can always be altered after you have created it, e.g. add or delete fields, alter the reports and so on.

Opening a blank database

Start a new file by clicking on the **New File** button on the toolbar.

Select **Blank Database** (**General**) and then **Create** it (giving it the name CUSTOMERS).

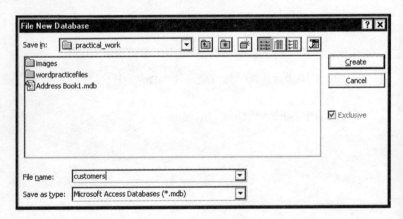

You will see the following screen, click on the **New** button.

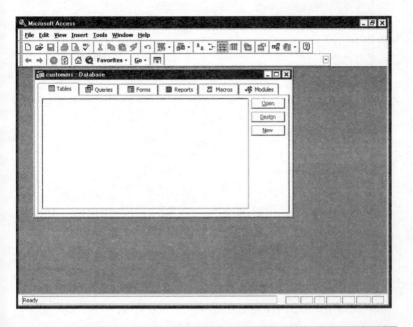

Tables are used to store the data, all other activities use the table as the data source.

Finally select **Design View** and click on the **OK** button.

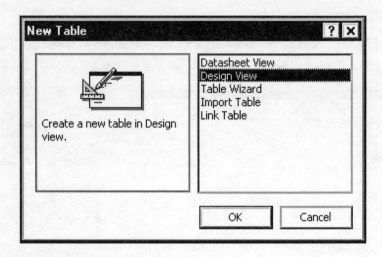

You can now decide upon the names and data type for the fields in your database.

To alter the **Data Type** from text, click on the arrow to the right and select from the pull down menu.

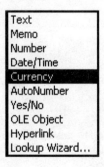

Enter the following details.

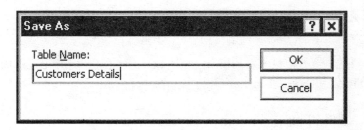

Field Name	Data Type
Company Name	Text
Address 1	Text
Address 2	Text
Town / Village	Text
County	Text
Postcode	Text
Date entered	Date/Time
Credit Limit	Currency

Close this down and save the table, giving it the name **Customers Details**.

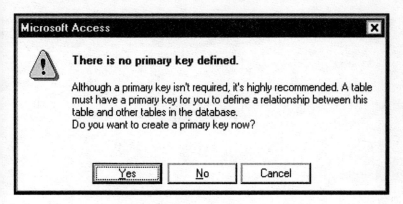

You will be asked if you want to create a primary key (this is the field used to organise the database).

> **Microsoft Access**
>
> **There is no primary key defined.**
>
> Although a primary key isn't required, it's highly recommended. A table must have a primary key for you to define a relationship between this table and other tables in the database.
> Do you want to create a primary key now?
>
> [Yes] [No] [Cancel]

Click on the **Yes** button and you should see the screen shown below.

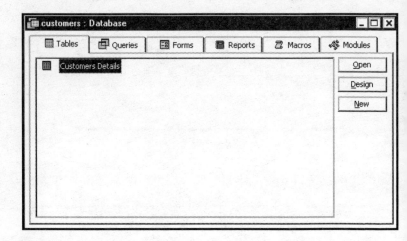

Click on the **Open** button and enter the following data (the **ID** is entered automatically by the program).

Use the **Tab** key to move onto the next field.

You must enter the **/** symbol in the date field (as shown below).

ID	Company Name	Address 1	Address 2	Town / Village	County	Postc ode	Date entered	Credit Limit
1	Fantastic Foods	The Old Mill	Brook Lane	Yeovilton	Somerset	BA65 8TR	24/12/97	£5,000.00
2	Lickable Ices	Station Road		Ilminster	Somerset	TA2 6YU	13/01/98	£7,000.00
3	Smashing Salads	Sunnyside	Jonah Close	Exeter	Devon	EX5 9EW	12/12/97	£3,000.00
4	Better Bakes	12 Dreadnought Avenue		Exmouth	Devon	EX7 4WS	14/02/96	£8,000.00

Finally, close all the files, saving any changes.

Adding data to a database

Open the file CUSTOMERS and then the table **Customers Details**.

Click on the next record and enter the new data.

ID	Company Name	Address 1	Address 2	Town / Village	County	Postcode	Date entered	Credit Limit
5	Delightful Donuts	Unit 4	Spring Park	Plymouth	Devon	PL6 8TR	23/05/94	£2,000.00
6	Exciting Edibles	87b High Street		Midsomer Norton	Somerset	TA45 7R	13/06/95	£3,500.00

Sorting the data

Pull down the **Records** menu; select **Filter** followed by **Advanced Filter/Sort**. You will see a new screen, enter the following details for **Field** and **Sort** by clicking in the box and then on the arrow symbol to the right of the box.

Field:	County	Company Name
Sort:	Ascending	Ascending
Criteria:		
or:		
◄		

Pull down the **Filter** menu and then **Apply Filter/Sort**, the data should be sorted by County and **within** County by Company Name.

ID	Company Name	Address 1	Address 2	Town / Village	County	Postcode	Date entered	Credit Limit
4	Better Bakes	12 Dreadnought Avenue		Exmouth	Devon	EX7 4WS	14/02/96	£8,000.00
5	Delightful Donuts	Unit 4	Spring Park	Plymouth	Devon	PL6 8TR	23/05/94	£2,000.00
3	Smashing Salads	Sunnyside	Jonah Close	Exeter	Devon	EX5 9EW	12/12/97	£3,000.00
6	Exciting Edibles	87b High Street		Midsomer Norton	Somerset	TA45 7R	13/06/95	£3,500.00
1	Fantastic Foods	The Old Mill	Brook Lane	Yeovilton	Somerset	BA65 8TR	24/12/97	£5,000.00
2	Lickable Ices	Station Road		Ilminster	Somerset	TA2 6YU	13/01/98	£7,000.00

Applying Filters

A filter lets you choose which parts of the database to display.

Pull down the **Records** menu; select **Filter** followed by **Advanced Filter/Sort**.

Type the word **Devon** in the **Criteria** under **County**, then pull down the **Filter** menu, and select **Apply Filter/Sort**.

Your database should now only display the companies in Devon.

ID	Company Name	Address 1	Address 2	Town / Village	County	Postcode	Date entered	Credit Limit
4	Better Bakes	12 Dreadnought Avenue		Exmouth	Devon	EX7 4WS	14/02/96	£8,000.00
5	Delightful Donuts	Unit 4	Spring Park	Plymouth	Devon	PL6 8TR	23/05/94	£2,000.00
3	Smashing Salads	Sunnyside	Jonah Close	Exeter	Devon	EX5 9EW	12/12/97	£3,000.00

Finally, pull down the **Records** menu and then **Remove Filter/Sort**. Your data should be back in its original state.

Close and (if prompted) save all the open files.

Forms

You can create a form for a variety of purposes, for example as a data entry form.

Open your **Customer** database, click on **Forms** and then **New**.

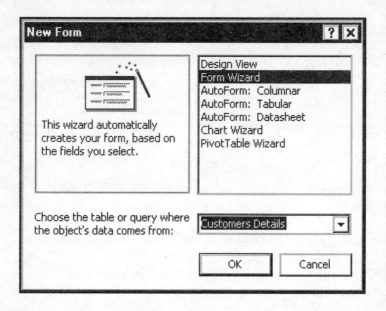

Choose the **Form Wizard** and **Customer Details** as the table or query.

On the next screen, click on the symbol to include all the fields in the form.

Carry on, choosing **Columnar** and then **Evergreen** on the next two screens.

Click on **Finish** and you will see the form displayed on the screen.

Maximise the window and you have a data entry screen which looks rather more professional than the **Datasheet** you used to enter the original data.

Click on the symbol at the bottom of the window to enter a new record and then enter the data shown below.

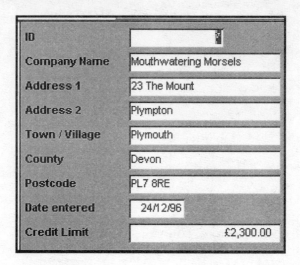

ID	
Company Name	Mouthwatering Morsels
Address 1	23 The Mount
Address 2	Plympton
Town / Village	Plymouth
County	Devon
Postcode	PL7 8RE
Date entered	24/12/96
Credit Limit	£2,300.00

Now close down this window and return to the original window.

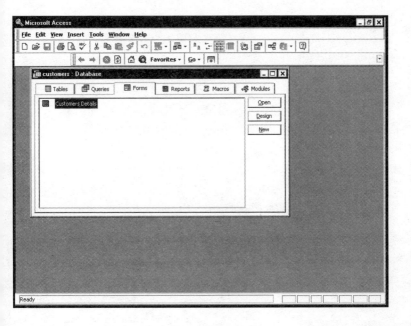

Reports

From this screen, select **Reports** and then **New**.

Choose the **Report Wizard** and **Customer Details** as the table or query.

Choose to enter all the fields into the report except for the **ID** and **Date entered** fields (use the single arrow button to enter each field.

On the next screen, group by **County** and then by **Credit Limit** by selecting the fields and clicking on the arrow.

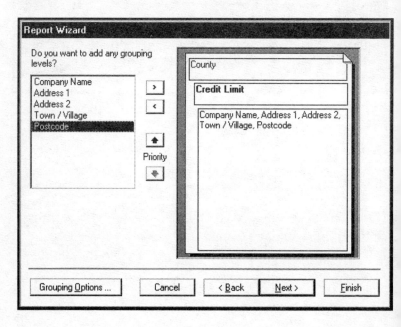

On the next screen, choose to sort by **Company Name**.

Choose **Landscape** (orientation) and **Stepped** layout and from the following screen **Soft Gray** style. Finally, click on **Finish** and you will see the report previewed on the screen.

Pull down the **View** menu, **Zoom** and **Fit to Window**. You will see the report as shown below.

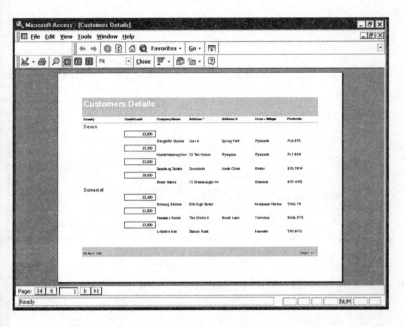

Unfortunately, all the data is not displayed (for example some of the Company Names are not shown in full).

Customising the report layout

Pull down the **View** menu and then **Design View**. You will see the design of the report.

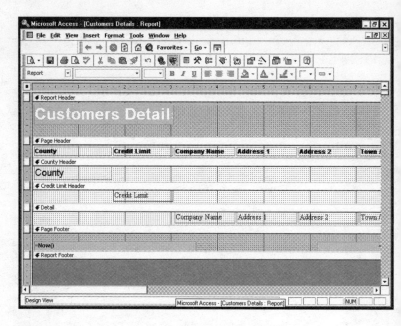

Increase the size of the **Detail** area by clicking and dragging the bottom of the area, then click, and drag the bottom of the **Customer Name** and **Address 1** boxes to make them bigger (the end result is shown below).

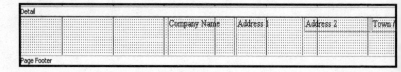

Close down the **Design View** window, saving the changes.

Click on the **Preview** button and pull down the **View** menu, **Zoom** and **Fit to Window**. You will see the report with all the data shown (if not, go through the process until it is).

Finally, close down all the open windows and close the file.

Practice

Open the CUSTOMERS database file and create a new **Table** (**New** followed by **Design View**).

The table should have fields and field types as shown below.

	Field Name	Data Type
🔑▶	Company Name	Text
	First Name	Text
	Last Name	Text
	Phone	Text
	Email	Text

Set the **Primary Key** after clicking in the **Company Name** field (**Edit** followed by **Primary Key**), and close the window, saving and calling the table **Contacts**.

Create a **New Form** (use the **Form Wizard**) using the **Contacts** table, include all the fields and whatever design features you want.

Use the form to enter the following data.

Company Name	First Name	Last Name	Phone	Email
Better Bakes	Julie	Harris	01935-65-3452	julieh@bb.net.com
Delightful Donuts	Donald	Dougan	0187-345654	donald.dougan@virginal.n
Exciting Edibles	Boris	Baskerville	0198-34-2345	boris.b@claris.net
Fantastic Foods	Cyril	Rakins	01786-761292	c.rakins@fast.net
Lickable Ices	Harry	Andrews	01543-65784	harryandrews@lices.com
Mouthwatering Morsels	Sally	Dodgy	0171-547865	sally.d@virginal.net
Smashing Salads	Fiona	Fortescue	01327-45632	fiona.fort@demons.net

Close the form.

Relationships between tables

You have now created two tables, **Customer Details** and **Contacts**. There is a common field (**Customer Name**) in each of the tables.

Creating the relationship

You should be looking at the **Database View** screen.

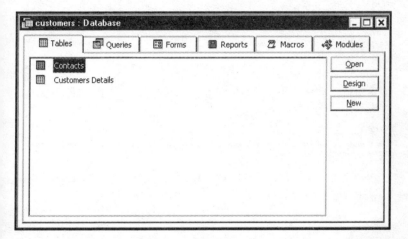

Now click on the **Relationships** button on the toolbar.

The following will appear.

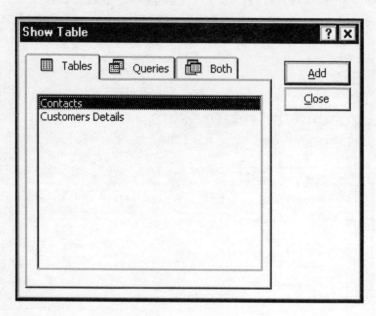

Click on each and then on the **Add** button (in turn) then click the **Close** button.

You should see the **Relationships** screen.

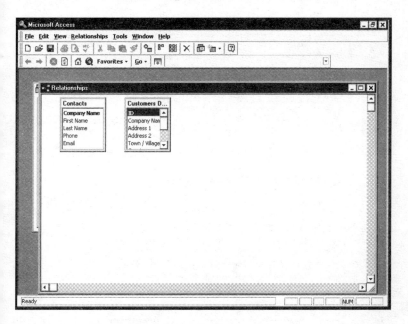

Click on the **Company Name** field in the **Customer Details** box and drag it to the **Company Name** in the **Contacts** box.

You will see the following dialog box, click on the **Create** button.

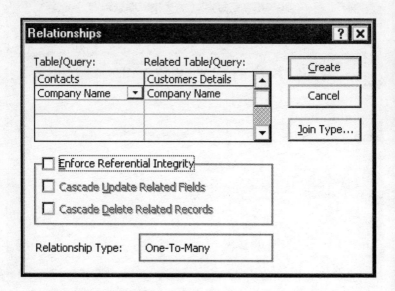

It is very important that the data is as shown above, if it is not then click on the arrows to alter the fields.

You should now see an arrow joining the two boxes; this means there is a relationship between them.

If you want to delete a relationship, click on the arrow so that it is bold and then press the **Delete** key.

Close down the **Relationships** window (saving the changes).

Queries

These are similar in nature to **Filters/Sort** within the **Records** menu with the difference that **Queries** can be used to look at data in related tables.

Click on the **Queries** tab and then on **New**.

Choose the **Design View** option and you should see this screen.

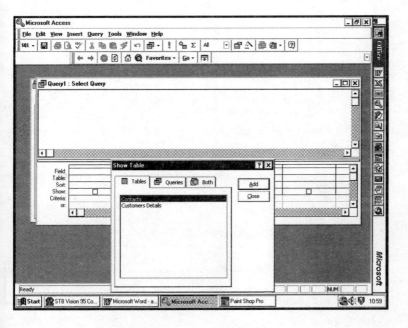

Select the **Contacts** table, then **Add**, finally **Close**.

Enter the fields shown below into the query.

Field:	Company Name	First Name	Last Name	Email
Table:	Contacts	Contacts	Contacts	Contacts
Sort:				
Show:	☑	☑	☑	☑
Criteria:				
or:				

Click on the **Show Table** button on the toolbar and **Add** the **Customer Details** table, then close the dialog box.

Add the **Credit Limit** field (this is the last field in the table) and **Sort** this (Descending).

Finally click on the **Run** button on the toolbar (to run the query) and you should see the following data.

Company Name	First Name	Last Name	Email	Credit Limi
Better Bakes	Julie	Harris	julieh@bb.net.com	£8,000.00
Lickable Ices	Harry	Andrews	harryandrews@lices.com	£7,000.00
Fantastic Foods	Cyril	Rakins	c.rakins@fast.net	£5,000.00
Exciting Edibles	Boris	Baskerville	boris.b@claris.net	£3,500.00
Smashing Salads	Fiona	Fortescue	fiona.fort@demons.net	£3,000.00
Mouthwatering Morsels	Sally	Dodgy	sally.d@virginal.net	£2,300.00
Delightful Donuts	Donald	Dougan	donald.dougan@virginal.net	£2,000.00

Finally, close down the query screens (saving the query as **Query1**).

Creating a report from a query

Once you have run a query you can create a report from the data contained therein.

To do so, click on the **Reports** tab and then **New**. Select **AutoReport: Columnar** and choose **Query1** as the table/query.

This will produce a report without you having to make any other choices.

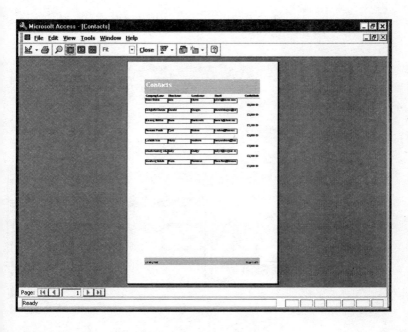

Close down the report windows and save the report as **Contacts**.

Extracting data from a database

You can use **Filters** and **Queries** to extract data from a database.

These can be used in a more sophisticated way than has already been covered; e.g., you can include criteria within the query.

Create a **New Query** using the **Simple Query Wizard**.

Include the fields shown below from the **Contacts** and **Customer Details** tables.

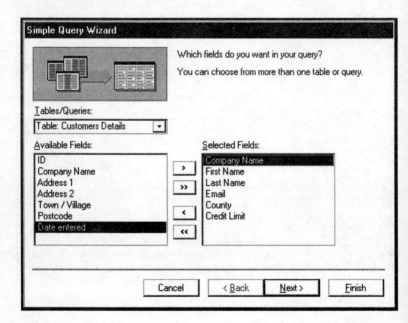

Accept the defaults for the rest of the screens and you should see the following result.

	Company Name	First Name	Last Name	Email	County	Credit Limi
▶	Better Bakes	Julie	Harris	julieh@bb.net.com	Devon	£8,000.00
	Delightful Donuts	Donald	Dougan	donald.dougan@virginal.net	Devon	£2,000.00
	Exciting Edibles	Boris	Baskerville	boris.b@claris.net	Somerset	£3,500.00
	Fantastic Foods	Cyril	Rakins	c.rakins@fast.net	Somerset	£5,000.00
	Lickable Ices	Harry	Andrews	harryandrews@lices.com	Somerset	£7,000.00
	Mouthwatering Morsels	Sally	Dodgy	sally.d@virginal.net	Devon	£2,300.00
	Smashing Salads	Fiona	Fortescue	fiona.fort@demons.net	Devon	£3,000.00
*						

Now pull down the **Records** menu and select **Filter**, then **Advanced Filter/Sort**.

Enter the following data.

Field:	County	Credit Limit
Sort:		Ascending
Criteria:	"Devon"	>2100
or:		

Finally, pull down the **Filter** menu and select **Apply Filter/Sort** and you will see the following.

	Company Name	First Name	Last Name	Email	County	Credit Limi
▶	Mouthwatering Morsels	Sally	Dodgy	sally.d@virginal.net	Devon	£2,300.00
	Smashing Salads	Fiona	Fortescue	fiona.fort@demons.net	Devon	£3,000.00
	Better Bakes	Julie	Harris	julieh@bb.net.com	Devon	£8,000.00
*						

Close down the window, saving it, it should be named **Contacts Query** (if it is not, then alter the name by clicking and overtyping).

Finally, to create a report based upon the filtered data and including a calculation:

Click on the **Reports** tab and then on **New**. Use the **Reports Wizard** and choose **Contacts Query** as the table/query to be used for the report.

Include all the fields.

Accept the next screens and then choose to sort by **Credit Limit**.

Choose **Landscape** orientation otherwise accept the defaults.

The result should look like this.

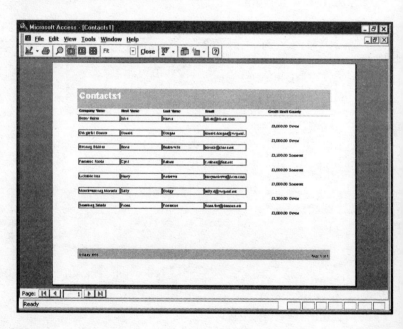

If some of the data does not fit, pull down the **View** menu and then **Design View**.

Manipulate the row widths and heights and the size/font of the headings and data boxes so that all the data is shown.

Go into **Design View** (**View** menu) and drag down the **Report Footer** until there is space to add text.

Drawing a text box

To do this, click on the **Toolbox** button on the toolbar. This will display the toolbox.

Click the **Text Box** button and drag to draw the text box.

Entering calculations into a text box

Once you have done this, click on the text box
to select it. Then click the **Properties** button on
the toolbar and on the **Control Source**

Click on the button on the far right, this will
load the **Expression Builder**.

Double-click the word **Functions** from the list and then
select **Built-In Functions**.

Choose the **Avg** function and click on the **Paste** button.

Highlight the **<<expr>>** in the top part of the box and then double click on **Queries**, followed by **Contacts Query** and **Credit Limit**.

Finally click on the **Paste** button.

At this stage, the **Expression Builder** should look like this.

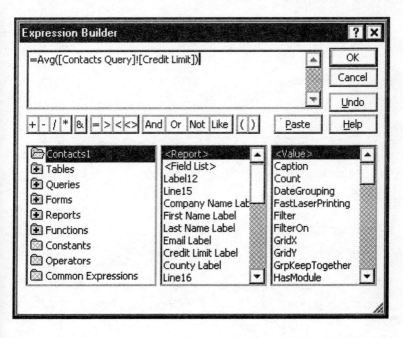

Click on the **OK** button to close down the **Expression Builder** window and the result should look like this:

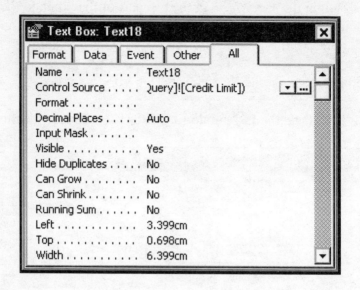

Close down this window and you will be back in **Design View**.

There should be an additional text box called **Text** (with a number). Delete this.

Click on the label button (in the toolbox) and draw a label box just before the calculated box.

Enter the following text:

Average Credit Limit = £

Line up the two boxes and click on the text box containing the calculation and then on the **Left** alignment button on the toolbar.

Pull down the **View** menu and select **Layout Preview**. You should see the text and the calculated average at the bottom of the page.

If the layout looks strange, go back to **Design View** and rearrange the label and text boxes as necessary.

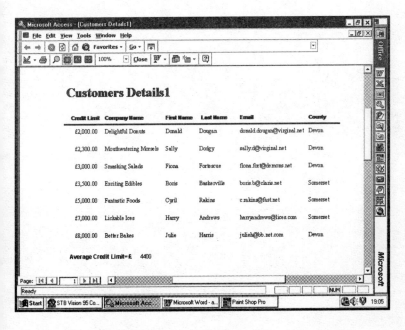

Close down all the open windows (saving the changes).

Appendices

The Standard Buttons

Microsoft Windows 95 lets you alter the size of the active window; there are four buttons, which appear on every window.

Clicking on this button closes down the program (you will be asked if you want to save any changes that you have made to the file).

This reduces the size of the window to its previous size. This button is an alternative to the next one.

This button enlarges the active (current) window to fill the screen.

This button minimises the window, if you do this you will see the program name appearing along the Windows 95 **Start bar** at the bottom of the screen. You can click on the program name to activate it.

Help

All Windows programs feature on-line **Help** that is valuable and easy to use, and makes both learning and problem solving easier.

All the programs have a **Help** pull down menu, the **Word** one is shown for reference.

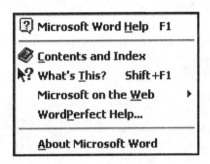

Contents and Index

You can access Help in three different ways, by using **Contents**, **Index** or **Find**.

Contents

This lists the topics (or books) which contain various hints, tips and explanatory information. Each of these books may contain sections or chapters within it. The screen from PowerPoint® is shown below.

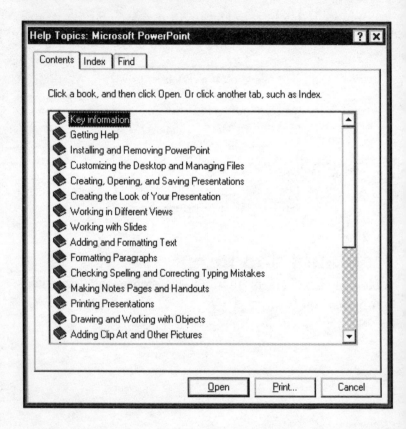

You can **Open** any of the books (by clicking on the topic and then on the **Open** button to see the chapters within), for example if you open **Working with Slides** then you can see all the topics under that heading.

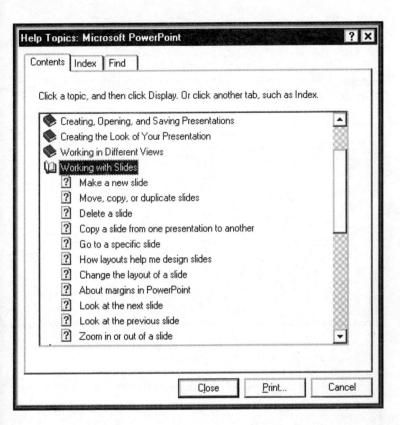

Select any of these (by clicking the mouse), then click on the **Display** button and all will be revealed.

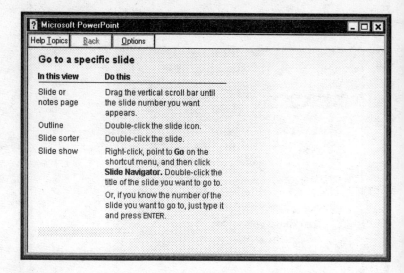

You can **Print** the topic instead of reading it on screen; this is especially useful if it is a complex activity.

Links to other Help screens are shown in green type, if you click on them (a hand should appear), you will see another Help screen explaining the relevant topic.

Index

You enter the first few letters of the topic you want to find
in the index. If the word or phrase does not exist then the
program will find the nearest equivalent (in spelling) to the
word you have entered.

Use the scroll bar or cursor keys to move up and down the
list.

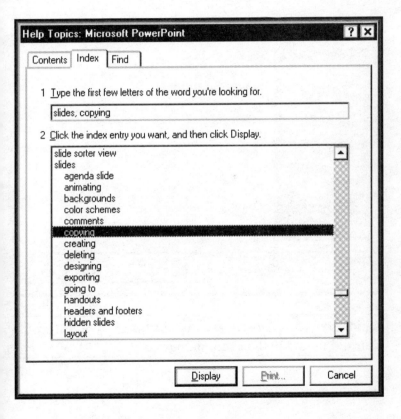

Once you have found the word or phrase you want help on,
click the **Display** button to see an explanation of the topic.

Find

The final option within Help is **Find**.

You enter the word or topic you want information on and the program will find it or the nearest equivalent.

The first time you use this, you will have to create a database and you will see the following screen.

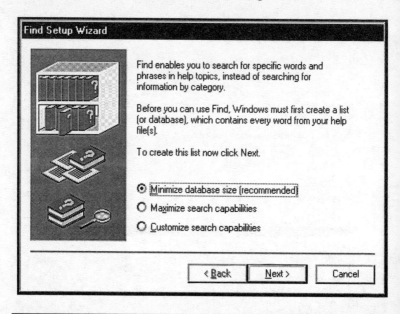

Whichever you choose you can adjust later by selecting the **Rebuild** button in the **Find** dialog box.

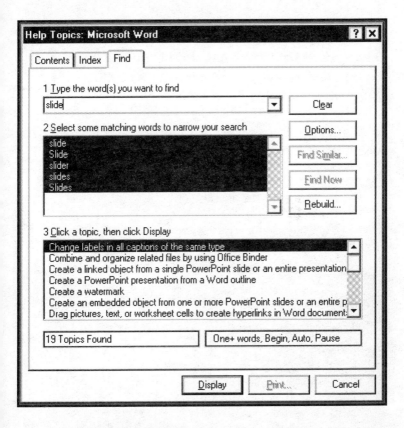

Often you will be presented with a list of items, select the one you want and **Display** the help connected with it.

Note the **Options** button, you can set parameters that are more precise for your search.

Find is probably the most sophisticated method of accessing information.

The Office Assistant

Do not forget the **Office Assistant** button on the toolbar. This is a quick and easy way of getting help.

An example of what happens when you click on the **Office Assistant** button is shown below.

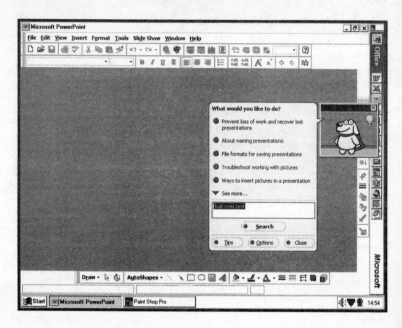

Working Efficiently

Whatever your computer system, you can maximise its efficiency by learning as much as possible about the way it works. Much of what you can do is beyond the scope of this book, however here are some ideas.

☐ Always save files to your **hard disc**, not to a floppy disc (except for backups). Hard discs are more reliable and much faster than floppies. The only uses for a floppy disc are for backup, for moving files from one physical location to another and for installing programs (although CD is replacing even this).

☐ Make sure that you have a **Swap** file installed (see Microsoft Windows 95 Control Panel, System, Performance, Virtual Memory).

☐ Ensure you have enough **RAM** memory. This is (relatively) cheap and can be more cost effective than a faster processor. This is particularly important if you intend to have several application programs and files open at any one time

Index

C

D

R

S

X

Z